IMAGES
of America

FIREFIGHTING IN WILLIMANTIC

On the Cover: The cover image is taken from a collection of photographs gathered throughout the years by fire department members. (Courtesy of the Willimantic Fire Department.)

IMAGES
of America

FIREFIGHTING IN WILLIMANTIC

Michael E. Tirone and Peter J. Zizka
Foreword by Marc A. Scrivener

ARCADIA
PUBLISHING

ISBN 978-0-7385-9293-0
Published by Arcadia Publishing
Charleston, South Carolina

Printed in the United States of America

Library of Congress Control Number: 2012935150

For all general information, please contact Arcadia Publishing:
Telephone 843-853-2070
Fax 843-853-0044
E-mail sales@arcadiapublishing.com
For customer service and orders:
Toll-Free 1-888-313-2665

Visit us on the Internet at www.arcadiapublishing.com

This book is dedicated to the generations of Willimantic firefighters who have served with loyalty, dedication, and pride.

CONTENTS

Foreword

The book you now hold in your hands represents not only the best collective history of the Willimantic Fire Department but also hundreds of hours of work by many people. Retired Norwich firefighter Michael Tirone, Peter Zizka—whose grandfather was a Willimantic mayor, firefighter and union president Ronald Lemire, firefighter Ronald Miles Jr., and most of the department's retirees were instrumental in completing this project, and we offer our sincerest gratitude.

As you look through these pages, I encourage you to visit some of the places where these historical events transpired. Let your imagination hear the alarm of "FIRE!" and the subsequent clatter of horses' hooves or the roar of an early motorized fire apparatus. See in your mind's eye the billows of smoke and the look of panic on the faces of people streaming from a burning building.

While you allow your imagination to recreate these events, I invite you to reflect on the legacy and example of courage, pride, sacrifice, and service given to us by the firefighters of years past, some whose sooty faces are captured on these pages.

After you have thoroughly explored the history of the Willimantic Fire Department on the pages of this book, and after you have visited some of these historical sites, I encourage you to walk over to 13 Bank Street. Meet some of the vigilant men and women who stand ready to lay down their lives to protect the citizens of Willimantic. Sit in the modern fire apparatus and have your photograph taken. Who knows, maybe your image will be included in some future anthology.

—Marc A. Scrivener
Fire Chief
Willimantic Fire Department

Acknowledgments

The authors would not have been able to complete this project without assistance and contributions from these people. Their input, encouragement, and donation of time and photographs have made this book what it is. We would like to acknowledge them here.

Current Willimantic fire chief Marc Scrivener; captains Ron Palmer Jr., Scott Card, Peter Smat, and Kevin Theriault; Ron Lemire, the firefighters union president; firefighters John Beck, Robert Golas, Peter Bruscato, Joseph Rijs, and Alberto Torres; and the rest of the men and women of the Willimantic Fire Department, who allowed us access to the photographs and artifacts inside the fire headquarters and assisted us in research.

Thank you to the retirees who were instrumental in contributing photographs and the stories that went with them, from the earlier times of the fire department. Those stories sometime took us off point but were important in our project. These men include the following: retired chiefs Ron Palmer Sr. and John Walsh; deputy chief Richard Miller; captains Joseph "Al" Beaulieu, Nick Lucas, Ed Lussier, and Richard Garneau; firefighters John Griffin, Robert and Gary Gorgone, Joseph Marsalisi, Fran Shea, Tony Santa Lucia, and Robert Theriault; and countless other retirees and their families, from far and wide. Even though they could not be directly involved, they gave their encouragement to us when our spirits were lagging. Special thanks go to Kevin Crosbie, publisher of the *Willimantic Chronicle*, for allowing us to use so many photographs and to borrow from so many *Chronicle* stories.

Other contributors were Butch Ives, a local collector of Willimantic memorabilia; Mayor Ernie Eldridge; members of the Willimantic Historical Society; and the staff of the Willimantic Textile Museum. To these and the many others we may have forgotten, our thanks to you for your contributions and encouragements, without which we would not have been able to complete this.

INTRODUCTION

Willimantic began in 1833 as a small borough of the town of Windham and was originally overshadowed by the more heavily settled and prosperous Windham Center. However, Willimantic was located on the river from which it took its name and, because of the amount of waterpower available, Willimantic grew rapidly into a mill town and began to be the center of activity in the town. The great number of mills in the town gave Willimantic the nickname Thread City.

Woven closely into the fabric of life in Thread City is its fire department, whose own beginnings mirrored the growth of the borough, which was incorporated as a city in 1893. Although there was a fire company in Windham, Willimantic had no fire protection organization of its own. And so, in 1830, the state legislature passed a resolution stating that "the civil authority and selectmen of said Windham may meet at Willimantic . . . and are hereby directed to nominate and form a Fire Company to work a fire engine for the protection of buildings in said village, and said town, from fire. [It] shall be called, '*The Willimantic Fire Engine Company*.'" In 1832, the company purchased an engine known as the Deluge. The engine house was located where the Jordan block—now the home of the Eastern Connecticut State University Foundation building—stands.

The first big fire was in 1842, when the Potter Tavern burned and two lives were lost. During the fire, the engine was put into service and a double line of townsfolk formed across the lots down to the Willimantic River, and water, passed along in pails, was poured into the engine. The site of the Potter Tavern later became home to Young's Hotel and then the Johnson House, which itself was almost completely destroyed by fire in 1915.

Several smaller fires occurred in the next few years, but the engine proved to be not as effective as hoped and the company disbanded in the 1850s. In 1868, the disastrous Franklin Hall fire, in which three business buildings were destroyed, renewed the public's attention to the need for firefighting facilities. An appointed committee received instructions to purchase a secondhand engine from Greenville—a section of Norwich—for $300. The engine was mounted on wheels and operated by levers pumped by about 20 men. It had a suction hose to draw water from wells or other sources.

The borough continued its quick growth and the need for improved fire protection led the borough to order two chemical fire extinguishers in 1872. With the arrival of the chemical extinguishers, two fire companies were formed—Fountain Fire Companies 1 and 2—with John Crawford and Samuel Hughes as their respective foremen. The borough also purchased a truck with both single and extension ladders, and the Excelsior Hook and Ladder Company was formed.

Within two years, the chemical extinguishers were replaced by hose wagons. Fountain Hose No. 1 became the Alert Hose Company No. 1, with its truck house approximate where Nathan Hale Hotel stands today. Fountain Hose No. 2 became Montgomery Hose Company No. 2, with its truck house on Union Street.

A lesser-known, short-lived unit, the Union Bucket Company was on Valley Street. Only a few brief newspaper reports bear testimony to its existence. Like the other fire companies, it responded to alarms of fires and, at other times, provided social events for the town, such as dances at Franklin Hall. It also had splendidly decorated rooms and participated in parades and other functions held by the fire companies of other towns. The Bucket Company came in handy several times when fires occurred out of range of the equipment of the hose companies. While local businessmen were generous to the company through donations of equipment, it went out of existence due to a lack of support from the borough's government.

The other companies, however, were well funded and well equipped. In 1887, the newly built Bank Street firehouse became home to the Alert Hose and Excelsior Hook and Ladder companies. A second new firehouse was built on Jackson Street to house the Montgomery Hose Company. The fire bell was rung for the first time on September 1, 1887, and it was noted that it had a "fine, clear tone that would attract peoples' attention." It replaced the bell on the Methodist church.

In April 1897, a large, fierce brushfire raged in the Hill Section. Alarmed residents sent word to Chief Charles E. Leonard, who, according to the *Willimantic Chronicle*, "took a force of eight men and a line of hose up the hill and put out the fire after considerable trouble." Subsequently, many residents of the Hill Section and some of the city's most prominent citizens petitioned for a new firehouse. After some hesitation by the city council, it was recommended that a volunteer fire company of 10 members be formed and a hose house be built for "less than $50." It took the name Hilltop Hose Company No. 3.

These first volunteer companies provided Willimantic with much more than fire protection. They were social clubs for their members and organized parties and parades, dinners and dances, fairs, functions, and fundraisers. In 1873 alone, "the Alerts" gave three balls. As the city of Willimantic grew, with an increasing number of mills and fine Victorian homes, so did the fire department.

A look through old city directories and the annual reports submitted by department heads provides a wealth of information about the department. The 1880 directory lists the companies as Excelsior Hook and Ladder, with foreman George Melony; Alert Hose Company No. 1, with foreman George Millard; Montgomery Hose Company No. 2, with foreman Luke Flynn; and the Union Bucket Company, with foreman John Leonard. Willimantic was divided into three fire districts, each one with an alarm box. The purpose of the fire alarm system at that time was to notify the three mills that furnished water for the hydrants to start their pumps. Two rounds from a box meant for the mills to start the pumps, and one round was the signal to stop. The bell at the Baptist church served a double duty as the city's fire bell.

By 1881, the Excelsior Hook and Ladder Company had its truck house at 191 Main Street—the current main office of the Savings Institute—and met on the first Thursday of each month. The Alert Hose Company had its truck house at 193 Main Street and met on the first Monday of each month. The Montgomery Hose Company was located at 29 Union Street. By this time, the city was divided into six fire districts, each of which had at least one fire alarm box.

In 1898, chief engineer Luke Flynn, in his annual report, recommended the purchase of 600 feet of rubber hose. He also commended department members for their "gentlemanly conduct and willingness to at all times respond to the call for the protection of life and property."

By 1900, Charles E. Leonard had become the chief engineer and the inspector of buildings. In his 1901 report, Chief Leonard mentioned that he had recommended, and the city had purchased, a new hook-and-ladder truck. The arrival of this first horse-drawn apparatus was a cause for celebration in the city. Chief Leonard said of the new truck, "A great many people have inspected it and we hear only words of praise for it, and it has been handled very successfully by the firemen." Chief Leonard reported in 1903 that a new building for the Hilltop Hose Company had been completed and, "the Hilltops feel very grateful and proud of their new quarters." That year, the department responded to seven alarms, mostly chimney fires, which resulted in losses amounting to $4,646.

In 1905, chief engineer James S. Donohue said that the department experienced greater activity during that year than at any other time in the history of the department. It responded to 22 alarms of fires, resulting in losses of $33,197.47. It should be noted that the chief engineers submitted meticulous reports. Each fire was listed in detail with the date, time, location, box number, owner, occupant, cause, loss of building and contents, and how much was covered by insurance. Chief Donohue also called for "two new hose trucks of standard make to take the place of those at present stationed in the Alert Hose Company and Montgomery Hose Company rooms." He said that the present ones had been in use since the organization of the department and were in a dilapidated condition due to "constant and hard use."

On July 1, 1917, the fire department transitioned from a volunteer to a paid department consisting of eight men. At the end of 1917, the department's apparatus included one combination American LaFrance engine, one Seagrave hook-and-ladder truck with 269 feet of ladders, one ladder truck with 126 feet of ladders, three American LaFrance combination chemical and hose wagons, and two hose reels. The fire alarm system were completely overhauled, and copper wire replaced the older iron wire. There were now 35 alarm boxes throughout the city.

In 1926, all four companies were combined in the Bank Street building. This was the beginning of a new era in Willimantic firefighting, from the iconic Bank Street headquarters. This structure stayed in service as the home of the Willimantic Fire Department until 1977, when because of space and old age, the fire department moved to its present quarters across the street, at the corner of Bank and Meadow Streets.

This book celebrates the history not just of a fire department, but of all the members who contributed so much to Willimantic throughout the years. From its beginning as a group of social clubs to its present-day highly trained and professional cadre, the Willimantic Fire Department has evolved in response to Willimantic's needs. Yet, throughout its nearly 150-year history, the department has never lost the spirit of camaraderie and connection to the community that has been its hallmark.

One

The Volunteer Era

An 1894 souvenir edition of the *Willimantic Journal* wrote glowingly about the 22-year-old department: "the superiority of its fire department is a feature of which the young city boasts and the people are loyal and generous in its support." At that time, the department had two firehouses—each with a hose tower—four four-wheel hose wagons, and a hook-and-ladder truck. The department consisted of a chief engineer, Charles Leonard, his three assistants, six fire police, and 100 firefighters. Other equipment included 3,500 feet of two-and-a-half-inch rubber-lined hose. The department never used steam fire engines because there were fire hydrants located throughout every part of the city. The department also had a Gamewell fire alarm system.

The members of the companies, affectionately called the "fire laddies" or "the boys," became the talk of the town. The events of each company—they were also known as the Alerts, the Excelsiors, the Monties, and the Hilltops—were closely followed by citizens and reporters alike. The companies sponsored dinners, dances, carnivals, parades, and even musicals at the Loomer Opera House.

The firehouses themselves were social centers for the members. It was said that the Alerts had decorated their rooms "in fine style," with mahogany-framed furniture. There were rich Brussels carpets, Smyrna rugs, and elegant drapery over the arched window. Statuary and gilt picture frames adorned the rooms as well. The rooms of all the companies also contained souvenirs from events celebrated with other fire companies.

Getting together frequently for social events, competitions, and parades, many fire companies developed long-term bonds with fire companies from different towns. Parades were always carefully planned and elaborate affairs, with the visiting fire company often bringing not just its entire membership but some of its equipment as well, usually by special train.

The four fire companies are seen here. From left to right, they are the hose wagon of Hilltop Hose Company, the ladder truck of Excelsior Hook and Ladder, the hose wagon of the Alert Hose Company, and the hose wagon of the Montgomery Hose Company.

The Bank Street headquarters was built in 1886. A year later, it became home to Hose Company No. 1 and the Excelsior Hook and Ladder Company. Note the "Alert" and "Excelsior" bricks above the keystones. Each company had room for their equipment on the truck house floor and a spacious parlor on the second floor. The original company had been located in the Walden and Griggs Block on Main Street.

The Bank Street headquarters is seen here with both doors open. The Alert Hose Company wagon is on the left, and the Excelsior Hook and Ladder is on the right. In 1887, the Excelsior Hook and Ladder moved from their Main Street building to Bank Street.

The Alerts decorated their business and reception rooms well, with easy chairs and a mahogany-framed "tete-a-tete." There were rich Brussels carpets, Smyrna rugs, and elegant drapery over the central arched window.

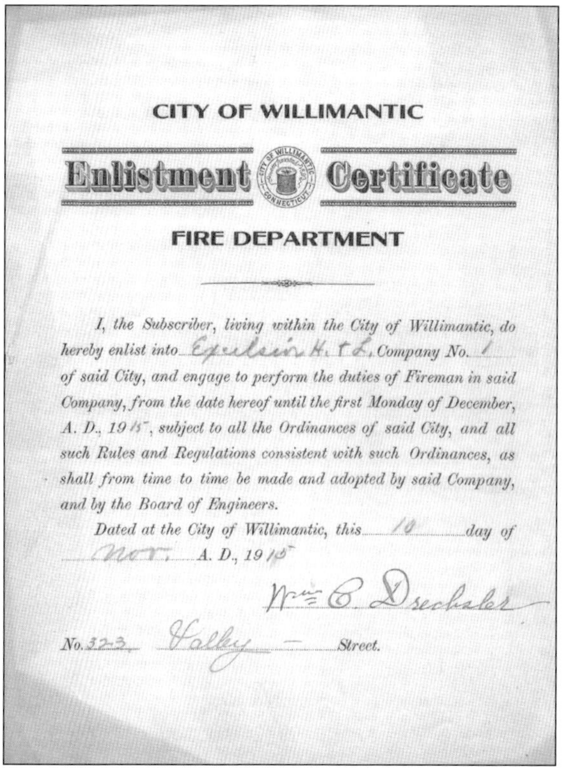

CITY OF WILLIMANTIC

Enlistment Certificate

FIRE DEPARTMENT

I, the Subscriber, living within the City of Willimantic, do hereby enlist into Excelsior H. & L. *Company No.* 1 *of said City, and engage to perform the duties of Fireman in said Company, from the date hereof until the first Monday of December, A. D., 19*15, *subject to all the Ordinances of said City, and all such Rules and Regulations consistent with such Ordinances, as shall from time to time be made and adopted by said Company, and by the Board of Engineers.*

Dated at the City of Willimantic, this 10 *day of* Nov. *A. D., 19*15

Wm C. Dreschler

No. 323 Valley *Street.*

The Alert Hose Company No. 1 Assembly Room on Bank Street is seen above in the 1890s. Like many other firehouses of the day, it was richly appointed, with a lovely billiard table, fine furniture, and carpeting.

This certificate of enlistment into the Excelsior Hook and Ladder Company is dated 1915. The requirements stated that the enlistee must reside within the city limits and be subject to the ordinances, rules, and regulations of the city and the officers. The name on the certificate is a Mr. Dreschler, residing at 323 Valley Street.

This formal photograph of the Excelsior Hook and Ladder Company is from 1907. In their 1908 "Souvenir and History," the "Hooks" wrote, "Many of the citizens who have achieved success, both in the business and professional fields, look back with pride and joy to the days when they ran to fires with the 'Hooks' and shaped their course 'Ever Upward.' "

In this formal photograph of the Alert Hose Company No. 1, only a few of the men appear to be looking straight at the camera. Also, a majority of the men sport mustaches and beards.

This is the Excelsior 1902 hook-and-ladder truck. Note the truss construction of the ladder wagon, the old-style leather helmets hanging off the truck, and the fire lanterns, axes, and hand fire extinguisher. This ladder truck only carried wooden ground ladders and did not have the elevating aerial that would come along in later years and needed only two horses instead of a four-horse team.

The first truck house for the Montgomery Hose Company was on Union Street. In 1886, Willimantic began building two new firehouses. The Montgomery's firehouse was dedicated in 1887, just a few months after the opening of the Bank Street firehouse. In this 1889 picture, the Montgomery Hose wagon sits in the doorway. Also visible are the "Montgomery" brickwork and the "2" on the door's keystone.

The members of the Montgomery Hose Company No. 2 pose for a formal photograph. Almost all members of this company were of Irish descent, and the story goes that it was named Montgomery in honor of early Irish patriot Richard Montgomery.

The Hilltop Hose Company No. 3 was organized in May 1897 after more than a decade of demands for fire protection from residents of "the Hill Section." They had little to work with. A small hose house measuring 10 by 12 feet was built near the corner of Chestnut and Summit Streets and housed a small, two-wheel apparatus.

In 1903, a new hose house was built. It was 28 feet by 36 feet and included the old hose house as an ell in the back. There were two large rooms on the second floor—a parlor and an assembly room. Hilltop Hose was now equipped with two hose wagons as well as the old Excelsior hook-and-ladder truck.

Hilltop Hose No. 3 celebrated its 20th anniversary in grand style. A banquet was held and remarks were made by Mayor Daniel P. Dunn, who complimented the firemen for their work. City leaders also gave short addresses. In this photograph from the 1917 celebration, the Hilltops gather in their dress shirts—red trimmed with white and the very prominent "3."

The "Hilltoppers" became quite active in many local organizations and leagues. This is the 1913 Hilltop championship bowling team. For several years, the YMCA hosted an intercity bowling league at its alleys. The "Hilltoppers" competed against seven other teams from organizations such as the Thread City Cyclers, the Grex Club, and the post office clerks.

The interior of the parlor of Hilltop Hose Company No. 3 is seen here in the 1880s. The room resembled the gentlemen's clubs of England, with rich appointments, nice furniture, and the like. Note the several spittoons, the piano, and the flooring and carpeting in this photograph.

Alert Hose Company members pose in civilian clothing with an advertisement for one of their many community events. Their casual poses denote an air of camaraderie. Hidden in the background is the Alert Hose wagon—the hose lamp is just visible in the center. The Alerts sponsored a multitude of events every year, including minstrel shows, which they performed in.

The Excelsior Hook and Ladder Company No. 1 is seen here. The men in dark uniform coats are the foreman and assistant foreman, the forerunners to the positions of either chief and/or company captain. The man with the pipe on the far right may have been the driver, or "first whip."

These late-1800s badges are from the early fire companies. The badges are called thumbnails and are worn on one's lapel when not in uniform.

Below, Alert Hose Company's new 1906 American-LaFrance hose wagon waits outside the Bank Street headquarters. It was a combination chemical and hose wagon with a 35-gallon chemical tank and almost 1,000 feet of regular hose. It also carried ladders, buckets, and pike poles. Even in the 19th century, the sight of a fire engine brought out children of all ages.

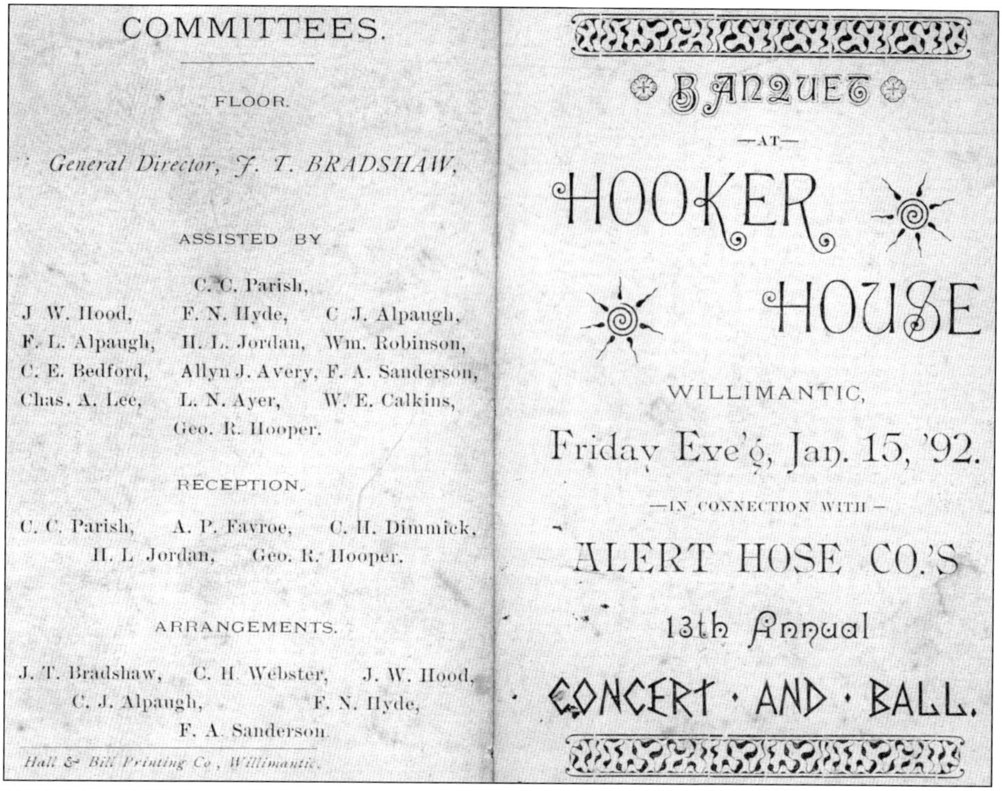

COMMITTEES.

FLOOR.

General Director, J. T. BRADSHAW,

ASSISTED BY

C. C. Parish,
J. W. Hood, F. N. Hyde, C. J. Alpaugh,
F. L. Alpaugh, H. L. Jordan, Wm. Robinson,
C. E. Bedford, Allyn J. Avery, F. A. Sanderson,
Chas. A. Lee, L. N. Ayer, W. E. Calkins,
Geo. R. Hooper.

RECEPTION.

C. C. Parish, A. P. Favroe, C. H. Dimmick,
H. L. Jordan, Geo. R. Hooper.

ARRANGEMENTS.

J. T. Bradshaw, C. H. Webster, J. W. Hood,
C. J. Alpaugh, F. N. Hyde,
F. A. Sanderson.

Hall & Bill Printing Co., Willimantic.

BANQUET

—AT—

HOOKER HOUSE

WILLIMANTIC,

Friday Eve'g, Jan. 15, '92.

—IN CONNECTION WITH—

ALERT HOSE CO.'S

13th Annual

CONCERT · AND · BALL.

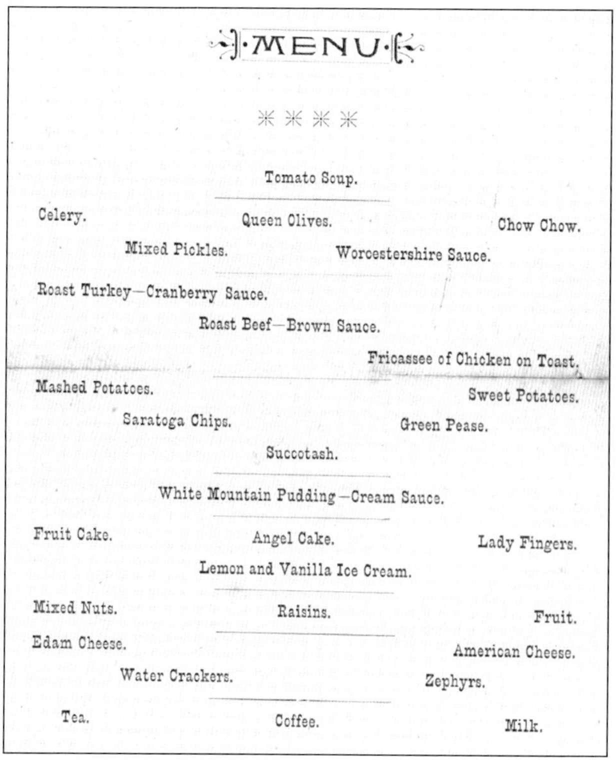

·MENU·

Tomato Soup.

Celery. Queen Olives. Chow Chow.

Mixed Pickles. Worcestershire Sauce.

Roast Turkey—Cranberry Sauce.

Roast Beef—Brown Sauce.

Fricassee of Chicken on Toast.

Mashed Potatoes. Sweet Potatoes.

Saratoga Chips. Green Pease.

Succotash.

White Mountain Pudding—Cream Sauce.

Fruit Cake. Angel Cake. Lady Fingers.

Lemon and Vanilla Ice Cream.

Mixed Nuts. Raisins. Fruit.

Edam Cheese. American Cheese.

Water Crackers. Zephyrs.

Tea. Coffee. Milk.

Alert Hose Company No. 1 had banquets and balls. These events were looked forward to and were the talk of the town, sometimes bringing in luminaries from the town and visitors from other fire companies.

It was considered an honor to be invited to one of these events. The food, music, and camaraderie were talked about for days and weeks later. This is a menu for a banquet.

On Labor Day 1903, the Konomoc Hose Company of New London held its annual outing in Willimantic. Here, in the Labor Day Parade, the Warren Drum Corps of Putnam escorts Alert Hose Company No. 1 up Bank Street as the companies prepare to march. Note the bell tower of the Bank Street headquarters.

The firemen's parade was part of the daylong celebration, and all of the companies participated. Even local government leaders joined in the march. Each company sported brand-new uniforms, and their hose carriages were appropriately decorated. Here, the Alert Hose Company passes by the town hall.

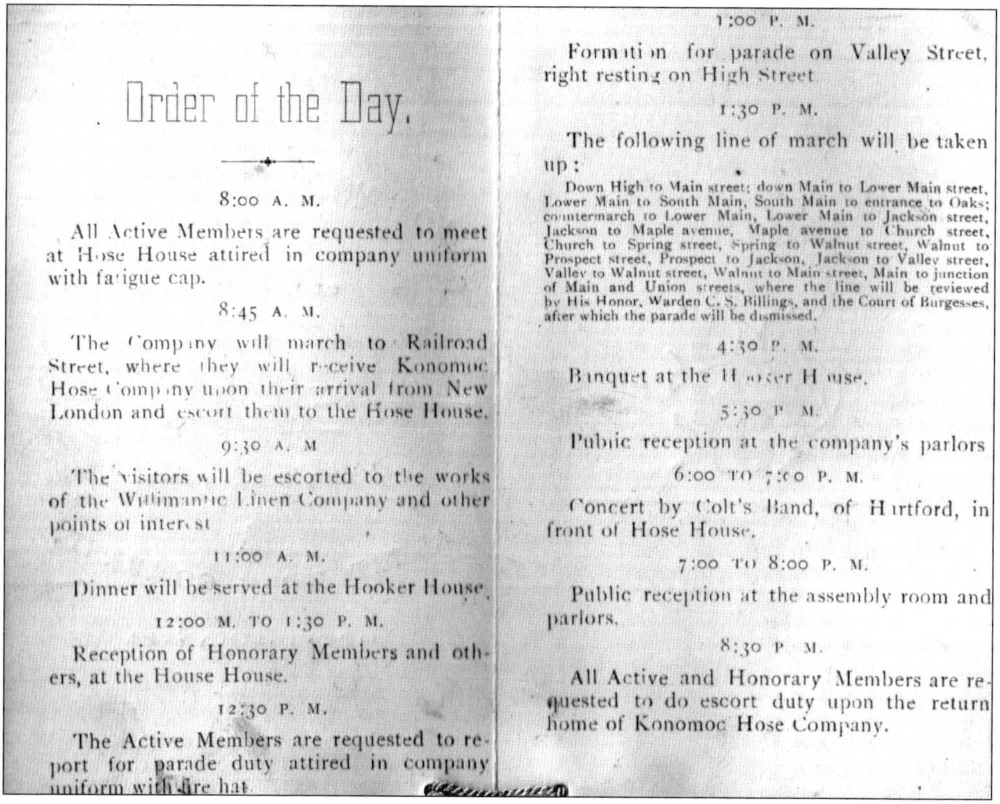

Order of the Day.

8:00 A. M.

All Active Members are requested to meet at Hose House attired in company uniform with fatigue cap.

8:45 A. M.

The Company will march to Railroad Street, where they will receive Konomoc Hose Company upon their arrival from New London and escort them to the Hose House.

9:30 A. M.

The visitors will be escorted to the works of the Willimantic Linen Company and other points of interest.

11:00 A. M.

Dinner will be served at the Hooker House.

12:00 M. TO 1:30 P. M.

Reception of Honorary Members and others, at the House House.

12:30 P. M.

The Active Members are requested to report for parade duty attired in company uniform with fire hat.

1:00 P. M.

Formation for parade on Valley Street, right resting on High Street.

1:30 P. M.

The following line of march will be taken up:

Down High to Main street; down Main to Lower Main street, Lower Main to South Main, South Main to entrance to Oaks; countermarch to Lower Main, Lower Main to Jackson street, Jackson to Maple avenue, Maple avenue to Church street, Church to Spring street, Spring to Walnut street, Walnut to Prospect street, Prospect to Jackson, Jackson to Valley street, Valley to Walnut street, Walnut to Main street, Main to junction of Main and Union streets, where the line will be reviewed by His Honor, Warden C. S. Billings, and the Court of Burgesses, after which the parade will be dismissed.

4:30 P. M.

Banquet at the Hooker House.

5:30 P. M.

Public reception at the company's parlors

6:00 TO 7:00 P. M.

Concert by Colt's Band, of Hartford, in front of Hose House.

7:00 TO 8:00 P. M.

Public reception at the assembly room and parlors.

8:30 P. M.

All Active and Honorary Members are requested to do escort duty upon the return home of Konomoc Hose Company.

Extensive preparations were always in the making when a visit from another fire company was expected. This "Order of the Day" from a previous Konomoc visit shows how the entire day was carefully planned. Note the long parade route that led back and forth through the city. The *Chronicle* article wrote that the Konomocs were "profuse in their thanks."

Newspaper accounts of the time offered rave reviews of the Alert's hose wagon and the spectacular way in which it was decorated. The Alerts decorated it in a different fashion for each parade.

The Alerts often traveled to other towns for parades. Here, they gather for a trip to New London to participate in a parade there. The Alerts, the Alerts Veterans Corps, and their specially decorated hose wagon traveled by special train after being escorted to the railroad station by the fire police and a marching band. (Photograph courtesy of Butch Ives.)

Alert Hose No. 1 members were guests of the Southington Hose Company. Note the inscription on top of the hose reel: "Thread City Boys." Willimantic was known as Thread City because of all the fabric mills there at the time.

The members of the Montgomery Hose Company No. 2 were the invited guests of the Niagara Hose Company No. 2 of Norwich. It was not uncommon for fire companies to travel to attend parades, balls, or other special events in other cities. This was done to show off a new apparatus or participate in the events. Here, ceremonial horns, dress uniforms, and ribbons adorn the Montgomery members.

The June 1915 Old Home and School Week Parade was part of what was called "Willimantic's biggest day." Here, past chiefs of the fire department ride in the parade. They were accompanied by all the department's apparatuses as well as the American Thread Fire Brigade and the South Windham Fire Department.

Two

THE PAID DEPARTMENT

On July 1, 1917, the fire department transitioned from a volunteer organization to a paid department consisting of eight men. The department took delivery of its first motorized apparatus in 1919. There were still horse-drawn rigs but motorized equipment eventually took over.

The auxiliaries were a group of men who supplemented the paid force. These auxiliaries had their own equipment provided by the civil defense program and were expected to be trained at the level of regular personnel. The high point of the auxiliary era was during the war years, when many men were overseas. When the war ended and men returned, the need for auxiliaries was not as acute. However, many of the auxiliaries made the progression to the paid force.

One major change in the modern years was the department's move from the ancient and cramped Bank Street headquarters to the new Public Safety Complex. This new home provided the department with the opportunity to expand its fleet of fire-suppression and emergency-response equipment.

This early 1920s photograph shows one of the department's first motorized fire apparatuses. Only two people are identified, Jeffrey Tighe (standing at far left) and Chief Garrick (standing second from right). With them is the fire mascot, an unnamed terrier.

Members of the Alert Hose Company pose with their new motorized apparatus. From left to right, they are E. Maneman, A. Barber, unidentified, Mr. Smith, H. Kelly, M. English, C. Reynolds, M. Sullivan, and E. Martin.

Pictured are fire chief Wade U. Webster and his driver. It is not known for sure whether this was his personal vehicle or the first fire chief's car. (Photograph courtesy of Butch Ives.)

Uniformed officers and civilian-clothed members pose together in this 1927 photograph. The man in uniform on the left is Mr. Garrick, who later became chief of the department.

This 1927 photograph shows Willimantic's Mack AC Bulldog hook-and-ladder truck. This was the state of the art in fire apparatus of the time, with a chain-drive transmission, a powerful engine, and a crank-powered elevating ladder. It carried a full supply of heavy wooden ground ladders, various other tools, and a tiller-operated back end, which enabled the long ladder to negotiate the narrow streets.

This 1927 photograph shows the brand-new Mack AC Bulldog engine, which featured a fire pump that could send hundreds of gallons of water per minute through hundreds of feet of fire hose. It could carry its own water supply with it, as well as much more equipment and manpower. This fire truck is now at the Connecticut Trolley Museum.

Fire department members posed for this photograph in the 1930s. They are, from left to right, Paul "Pop" Miller, Ray Sullivan, unidentified, Capt. Jeffrey Tighe, Lt. Henry Kelly, and three unidentified men.

Both old and new fire apparatuses are seen here in front of the Bank Street station. Standing in front of WFD 1 are Mayor James Hurley (right) and John Roy, the fire committee chair. The two uniformed men standing are fire chief Charles Reynolds (left) and assistant chief Roger English.

Firefighters made yearly visits to decorate the graves of their deceased comrades. From right to left are (first row) William Smith, Russell Taylor, Ray Sullivan, Francis O'Brien, and Mr. King; (second row) Ed Shepaum, George Thompson, unidentified, Paul "Pop" Miller, and George Menditto.

Operation Willimantic Plan was a huge Civil Defense exercise held in June 1953. It involved 1,400 firefighters, police, and communication workers who fought six mock fires set off by a simulated atomic bomb attack. In this photograph, a "victim" is lowered from the window of the William Brand Company on Valley Street.

These fire apparatuses include, from left to right, a fire auxiliary vehicle, Engine No. 3, and Truck No. 1. Mayor Florimond Bergeron, in the white shirt, stands on Engine No. 3. Smiling fire chief Leo Rivard points at the mayor. Duke, the fire dog, sits in the front seat of Truck No. 1.

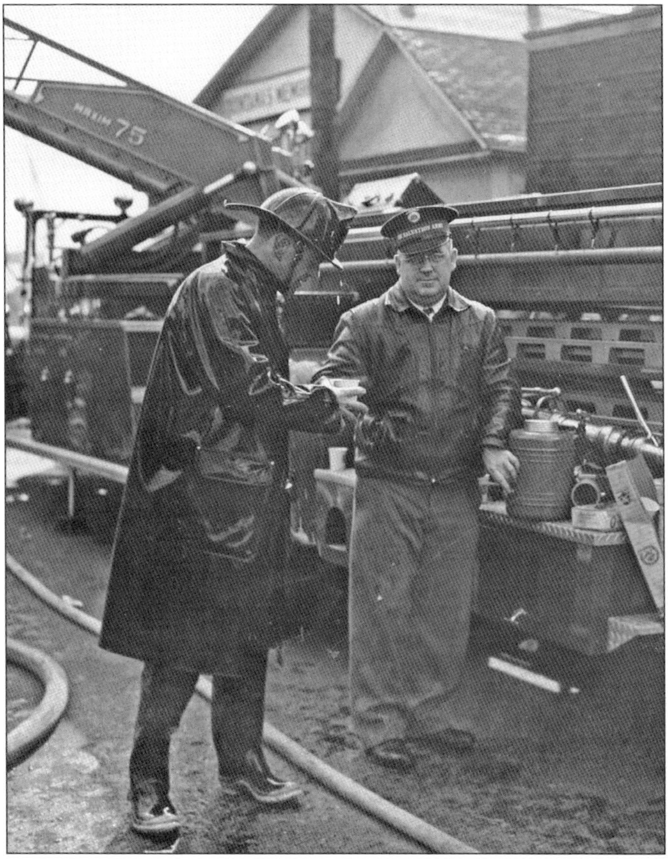

Firefighter Bill Nichols gets a cup of coffee from Salvation Army personnel after fighting a tough fire at Lindy's Restaurant in 1953. The Salvation Army canteen provided coffee at almost all major fires and was especially welcome at this one since it occurred on a cold, blustery March day. Bill Nichols later became fire chief.

The Willimantic auxiliary members are seen here in the 1940s. The auxiliaries had their own vehicle and even a portable pump, purchased with Civil Defense money. Here, they undergo pump and hose training at the American Thread. Some former members of the fire department, including retired firefighter Joseph Marsalisi, started as auxiliary and moved up to the regular ranks.

The auxiliary members gather at the Willimantic River behind the Thread Mill for pump training with one of the department's Ford V-8 pumps. The auxiliary fireman program began as part of Willimantic's participation in the Civil Defense programs begun right after the onset of World War II. Training in first aid and rescue techniques was also a part of this program.

Auxiliary members gather for a group photograph after a training exercise at the American Thread Company. The members took great pride in their equipment and their affiliation with the fire department; one member is polishing the fender of the auxiliary's vehicle.

The fire auxiliary vehicle is seen here in front of the Bank Street headquarters in 1942. Trucks and pumps similar to this were donated to departments all over the United States. The vehicles carried ladders, two lengths of hard suction hose, and several reels of 2.5-inch hose. The equipment was meant for exterior firefighting.

The auxiliary firefighters gather with Mayor Florimond Bergeron (standing at far left) and fire chief Leo Rivard (kneeling, in white coat) during the pump test for the new Engine No. 1. At that time, the fire department worked closely with Civil Defense authorities to ensure that we were prepared for any emergencies. These auxiliary members are wearing Civil Defense helmets.

Seen here in the late 1940s are, from left to right, the 1947 Rescue truck (partially hidden), Engine No. 3, the auxiliary company vehicle, and Engine No. 1. Engine No. 3 came to the fire department in 1943 with wooden bumpers because chrome and other metals were in short supply due to war requirements. The engine was eventually fitted with a chrome bumper.

In the 1960s, firefighters dedicated a plaque in memory of former members who had died. During the dedication, local clergymen blessed the plaque. Above, from left to right, are Rabbi Amos Edelheit, Fr. James Curry, firefighter George Menditto, fire chief Leo Rivard, firefighter Paul "Pop" Miller, and Rev. William Belury. The plaque is seen at right where it rests today in an enclosed case at the firehouse.

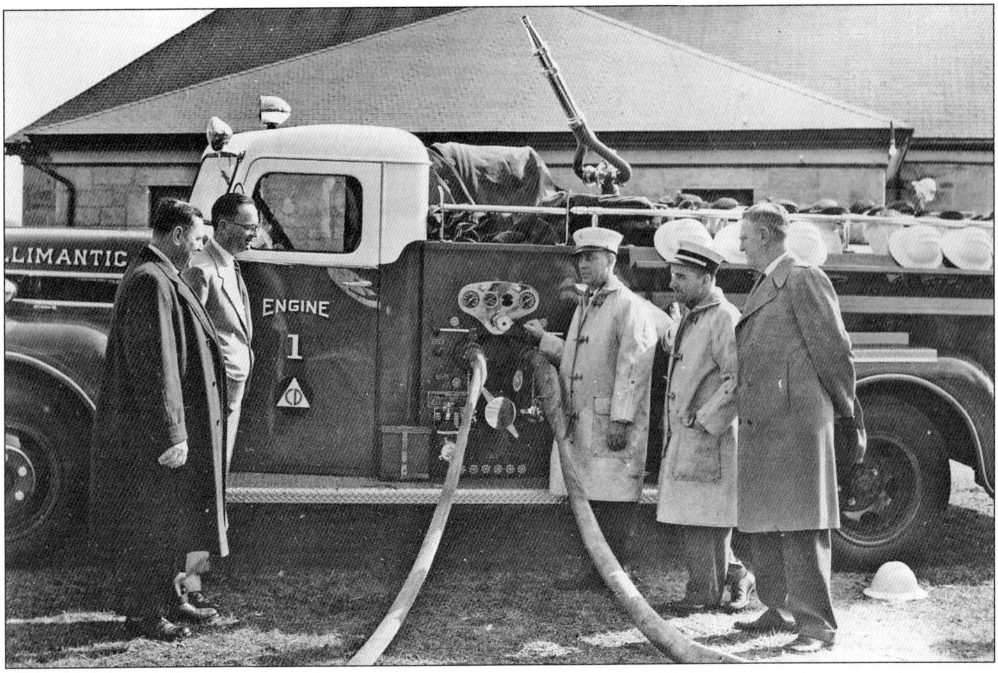

The newly purchased Engine No. 1 undergoes a pump test in 1953 prior to its commissioning. From left to right are Mayor Florimond Bergeron, Civil Defense Director Francis Barrett, fire chief Leo Rivard, deputy chief Albert Martin, and an unidentified man. Note the old Civil Defense shield on the door. When cities were given CD funds to purchase equipment—in this case, for half of the engine's $18,000 cost—having the shield on the door was a must.

Before an engine was commissioned, the fire department performed pump tests to ensure that it met specifications. This 1953 Maxim had a 500-gallon tank and a 750-gallon-per-minute pump. The pump test checked for the pump's capacity, pressure, and volume using different types of nozzles. The vehicle on the left is from Mansfield.

Willimantic Engine No. 1 passed its pump test and is seen here en route to a call at the corner of Jackson and Valley Streets. Many people still remember when there were sirens and red light globes mounted above the alarm boxes along Valley Street to warn pedestrians and motorists that fire trucks were approaching.

Alarm 1 is shown at a fire location in the late 1960s. From left to right are Milton Shippee, Lt. Charles Kelley, William Smith, George Taylor, and Russell Taylor (on ladder). Alarm 1 was used to maintain the fire alarm box system within the city.

Firefighter William Smith drives the 1951 Maxim Aerial 1 in 1964. This aerial was the primary ladder truck until 1978, when it was replaced by the 100-foot Maxim. It stayed in service as the reserve ladder into the 1980s, when it was finally retired permanently. It was then purchased by a private collector and is still driven in local parades.

In June 1964, the building housing Welch's Restaurant was badly damaged by a fire that was later attributed to faulty wiring. The upper floors of the structure had previously been condemned. At the time of the fire, the site was already being considered by the city as the location for a new public library, and the Willimantic Public Library was subsequently built there.

On May 18, 1970, a fire caused one death and destroyed two houses on Temple Street. A total of 43 residents were displaced. The first firefighters on the scene found the house at 29 Temple Street to be fully involved and the flames had already spread to the house at 27 Temple Street. A third house at 28 Center Street had some fire damage, as well.

Firemen were not able to enter 29 Temple Street, due to the intense flames and heat. Willimantic's Platoon 1 was the first on the scene and the other platoons arrived shortly thereafter, along with mutual aid help from North Windham and South Windham. Other departments assisted by providing air packs to be used by firefighters dealing with heavy smoke conditions.

Fire chief Ambrose Roy investigates the Temple Street fire. He determined the blaze to have been caused by a faulty oil burner in the basement apartment of 29 Temple Street.

In March 1978, a fire broke out on the third floor of the 115-year-old Elms Hotel. Fire officials believe the fire started when a mattress was ignited by either a match or a cigarette in one of the hotel's 40 rooms. When firefighters arrived at the 4:00 a.m. blaze, they were able to evacuate almost all of the building's residents, but one tenant died and two more tenants and a firefighter were injured.

In February 1974, fire completely destroyed an abandoned three-story house on Jackson Place. When firemen arrived, the house was already fully involved and the fire had spread to a neighboring two-story house. Firefighters got the fire under control in two hours. Here, firefighter Andrew Adamcik operates the pump.

In May 1975, fire gutted a three-story house on Elm Street. The house was fully involved when firefighters arrived. Firefighters Fran Shea and Jim Connell are on the ladder. On the ground are firefighters Tony Santa Lucia and Capt. Ed Lussier.

Firefighters Fran Shea and Jim Connell pour water on the blaze as the smoke pours out. Shea suffered from smoke inhalation and was taken to the hospital for treatment. Fire chief Patrick Cormier commended the firefighters for their hard work in keeping the fire contained to one building, since another building was only three feet away.

During a fire at the Heller Block on Main Street, firefighter Francis O'Brien (in full gear) and Lt. Charles Kelley help a victim down the ladder. The Heller Block was built in 1880 by Levi Frink, who was, according to the *Chronicle*, "a dealer and jobber in stoves, tin, glass, crockery and wooden ware." It was demolished in 1970.

Firefighter David Maynard sits on a window ledge after getting debris in his eye. This stubborn fire occurred at a three-story frame house on Natchaug Street in July 1992. The house was destroyed by the massive fire, and the intense heat blew out windows. A total of 11 people were left homeless by the blaze.

Firefighters Jack Pickett (left) and Nick Lucas prepare to enter a through a smoky second-floor window at a house fire on Keating Street in the 1970s. The home appears to have been abandoned, as evidenced by the plywood covering the windows.

For many years, firefighters decorated the Bank Street headquarters for Christmas. Here, there is a white cross in the center of the building. The firefighters who placed the lights on the building for this yearly tradition recall that it was not always easy work; sometimes they had to drop what they were doing and move the department's "cherry-picker" alarm truck for an emergency run.

The construction site of the present Public Safety Complex is seen here in 1976. Originally planned to be 37,000 square feet, it was trimmed to 33,000 square feet. The original target date for opening the complex was March 1977, but it was delayed until May.

The $2.3-million complex was formally dedicated in May 1977. Dignitaries attending included Sen. Christopher Dodd and state senator Audrey Beck. Fire chief William Nichols was presented with the book *San Francisco Firehouse Favorites*. It is uncertain if any of the recipes were ever tried.

This is the last group photograph to be taken before the demolition of the old Bank Street firehouse and the move to the new quarters. The department included, from left to right, (first row) Chief William Nichols, Capt. George Taylor, Capt. Ed Lussier, Capt. Walter Safin, and Capt. Bert Koppisch; (second row) firefighters Raymond Crosthwaite, Larry Lemire, Milton Shippee,

Joseph "Al" Beaulieu, Francis Shea, and Wayne Maheu; (third row) Robert Theriault, Anthony Santa Lucia, Roy Dingler, Richard Miller, Joseph DeMarchi, and John Griffin; (fourth row) Ron Palmer Sr., Jack Pickett, Nick Lucas, James Connell, Michael Bernat, Richard Garneau, Joseph Marsalisi, and Robert Gorgone.

Leaving the old station for the last time in late 1977, Capt. Milton Shippee (in shadow) takes a nostalgic last look as two other firefighters carry equipment to the new fire station. The Bank Street headquarters, the fire department's home for 90 years, was no longer large enough to accommodate the equipment needed by the department but it was filled with memories.

In April 1973, fire destroyed a building housing a grocery store and four apartments on lower Main Street. The six-alarm fire was brought under control in two hours. It occurred in a heavily populated area and drew a crowd of people. Firefighting efforts were hampered as a group of children rode bikes over fire hoses and dodged between fire trucks.

Capt. Ron Palmer Sr. surveys the scene of a fire on Jackson Street and Terry Avenue in the 1980s. It was a cold day—note the ice accumulation on the wires and trees.

On April 25, 1993, a five-alarm fire destroyed the building that housed the College Shoppe Luncheonette and Durand's Barber Shop on Ives Street. Residents of one apartment escaped from the building. Neighbors then called in the alarm and went into the building, helping the two residents of another apartment to safety.

Flames occasionally shot 10 feet and more above the roof and thick clouds of smoke billowed from the building on Ives Street. In this photograph, firefighters begin to evacuate the building as the roof flares up, igniting fears of a flashover that could cause potential harm to the men.

The helmet and gloves of a Willimantic firefighter rest on the hood of a rescue vehicle on Monday morning after the fire on Ives Street that began Sunday at 10:00 p.m.

Above, a firefighter cuts holes in the roof of the building from off the aerial ladder during this February 1992 fire at Young's Package Store. These duplex-style buildings, also known as mill houses, were common in this area of the city, having been built to house workers at the American Thread mill.

On October 12, 1994, a fire at 35 Arnold's Lane left seven people temporarily homeless. No one was home when the fire broke out, but one of the residents, returning from shopping, noticed that smoke was pouring out of a second-floor stairwell. Firefighters had the fire under control in less than 30 minutes and were able to rescue a small dog and three cats.

After the Arnold's Lane fire was out, three cats were unaccounted for, so firefighters went around the house and scooped up the cats, which had scurried underneath beds. Capt. Joseph "Al" Beaulieu holds one of the cats as firefighter Robert Gorgone and deputy chief Richard Miller follow.

One of the unusual duties of firefighting is rescuing animals, and firefighters are usually quite modest when talking about these selfless acts. In this 1989 photograph, Capt. Nick Lucas, showing the strain of a difficult firefighting task, still found the time to return a helmet full of rescued kittens to their obviously grateful and relieved caregivers. The $70,000 Milk Street fire seen here was started by a child playing with matches.

Above, firefighters prepare to enter the Hooker House hotel to fight a June 1970 fire. It began in a top-floor room and firefighters were able to contain it to the adjoining rooms. Firefighters used their aerial ladder to access a window and vent the room. The building was being used as a dormitory for Eastern Connecticut State University (ECSU) students.

At right, firefighter Ron Palmer Sr. endures not only flames and smoke but showers of sparks and water as he climbs to the roof of an apartment on West Avenue during this October 1988 fire. A total of 30 people were evacuated from nearby apartments, as the fire spread rapidly through the roof to adjoining units.

Because all other units were tied up at different calls, only one firefighter, Robert Theriault, was dispatched to a report of a fire in July 1993 at Northeast Recyclers. Upon arrival, Theriault faced a raging blaze and radioed to headquarters for a box alarm to be struck for additional assistance.

Firefighter Theriault began to set up equipment until backup arrived. The fire was believed to have started from a lightning strike to the roof of the building. Although there was extensive damage to the roof area, firefighters were able to keep the fire from spreading and had the blaze under control in less than an hour.

Spectators watch as firefighters battle a blaze that destroyed a three-story house on Windham Road in September 1995. The balloon-frame house went up in flames rapidly once the fire got into the walls. The firefighters began with an interior attack but were later pulled out of the house for fear of a flashover. The fire was brought under control in about 90 minutes.

Firefighters responding to this 1984 fire on Chapman Street found three separate fires burning. Firefighters inside and outside the building had to endure billowing smoke and the building was a total loss.

This 2001 aerial photograph of the Willimantic Fire Department's equipment shows, from left to right, Rescue 601, Engine 301, Truck 101, Tower 101, Engine 201, Rescue 101, and Rescue 501. After the attacks of September 11, 2001, many departments also received funding for special hazard vehicles. (Photograph courtesy of Firefighter Peter Bruscato.)

On October 22, 2002, an alarm from Box 24 brought firefighters to this fire on Pleasant Street. A second engine and truck responded with six off-duty firefighters less than four minutes after the box was struck. (Photograph courtesy of Scott Duplisea.)

In May 2000, a three-alarm fire occurred on Capen Lane. Despite a three-minute response time, firefighters Scott Card and Kevin Theriault of Platoon 2 arrived to find the house fully engulfed in flames. Because of the narrowness of the street, fire equipment could not get close enough to the house and firefighters had to drag hoses and ladders from Chapman Street.

Firefighters were called to a fire on the second floor at St. Joseph's Rectory. The church staff was alerted to the fire by an altar boy who had been sent to the rectory to get paperwork and saw smoke.

Local government leaders and prominent business leaders often joined with the fire department in support of its activities. Here, deputy chief Al Martin stands by as Mayor Florimond Bergeron sits atop a steamer fire engine supplied by Republic Oil and pulled by a team of horses from the C.C. Lounsbury Company prior to joining in one of the city's parades. (Photograph courtesy of Joseph "Al" Beaulieu.)

A March 2004 fire destroyed several townhouse units in the Cameo Gardens apartment complex. Fire chief John Walsh said that firefighters arrived within three minutes, saw heavy smoke and flames, and immediately called in a second alarm. A third alarm was later called in and Chief Walsh said that it took firefighters about three hours to extinguish the blaze.

This aerial shot shows the extent of the firefighting operation at the Cameo Gardens complex. The fire destroyed the unit it started in as well as three others. The apartment complex was built in the 1960s, before building codes called for fire barriers between units in the attic. Once the fire reached the attic, it spread across the top of the L-shaped building.

Ed Lussier (center, with Susie the dog) remembers that on the day of his promotion to captain, his platoon had a small going-away party with a cake for him. Two others in his platoon also went on to become captains. From left to right are (first row) Raymond Crosthwaite, Ed Lussier, and George Taylor; (second row) Robert Gorgone, Anthony Santa Lucia, Joseph DeMarchi, and Robert Theriault.

By the time Capt. Joseph "Al" Beaulieu (right), seen here receiving his helmet from fire chief John Walsh, was promoted in 1993, the ceremonies had become a little more formal than they were in Ed Lussier's day. Families and town leaders were invited to the ceremony, which was held in the department's conference room.

On November 4, 1994, Ron Palmer Sr., who had been with the department since 1972 and had been training officer since 1988, was promoted to captain. In this photograph, he hugs his daughter Hannah as his son Ron Jr. pins on his badge. Ron Palmer Jr. went on to become a captain in the department.

Three
Memorable Fires

The fire at the Melony Block became memorable because of the number of photographs taken of the city's horse-drawn equipment, which were later made into postcards. The Windham High School fire brought gloom to the city, as its beloved high school was lost. The Natchaug Garage, Thread City Garage, and Johnson House Hotel fire was memorable simply because of the sheer magnitude of loss. The Jordan Block fire and the subsequent demolition, which resulted in injuries and death, came just before the fire department became a paid department.

Later fires such as the Willimantic Lumber fire, the December 1944 fire, and the fires at the Shell Chateau, Lincoln Square on Valentine's Day, and the American Thread are memorable because of the amount of devastation they caused. The fires at St. Mary's School and the Normal School galvanized the community into action to rebuild the schools that were so important to so many.

The fire at Lounsbury's Garage brought debilitating injuries to Leo Theriault, a firefighter and decorated war veteran, and the fire department and the community rallied together to assist him. The fire on West Avenue, which led to the deaths of five children, wrenched the hearts of the firefighters on the scene and the community.

From the early times of horse-drawn apparatuses to the motorized era, these fires are the ones that many still speak of to this day.

The Melony Block fire occurred on May 6, 1908. The Maverick Laundry was located in the building, which was just across the street from the Hooker House hotel. At the time of the alarm, thick black smoke was coming from the building. According to the *Chronicle*, "some companies arrived very shortly after the alarm and in a few minutes there were three streams of water on the flames."

The fire was believed to have started in the basement drying room, where the combination of a large amount of clothes drying with carpets and oily machinery created not only a mass of flames but billowing clouds of smoke as well. Several firefighters were overcome and had to be helped back out. After getting some air, they were revived.

Because of the diligence of the firefighters, what at first looked like a disastrous fire was under control in about 40 minutes, after which firefighters began to take out baskets of clothes, some scorched and some merely wet. The recall was sounded at 1:05 p.m., just an hour after the original alarm.

On May 11, 1908, five days after the Melony Block fire, an article in the *Hartford Courant* stated that there was some criticism about the fact that there was a delay in getting apparatuses to the fire because it was necessary to wait for horses to draw the apparatus. Fire chief Wade Webster said it was just four minutes from the time of the alarm to the time that water was being sprayed on the fire.

Chief Webster continued to defend the horse-drawn equipment, saying that the apparatus got there as quickly as possible but that men were "distributed all over the city." The chief also lamented the fact that there was not enough equipment—rubber boots or coats—for all the firefighters and that the board of engineers had no rubber clothing provided to them by the city.

At 2:40 a.m. on April 28, 1913, a fire was discovered at Windham High School. The companies responded promptly, but when firefighters reached the school, it was apparent that the fire had progressed rapidly. The heat was so intense that firemen working the nozzles had to be covered with wet blankets. Crowds soon gathered from the city and surrounding areas.

At the height of the blaze, there were several explosions from the chemistry laboratory. Pieces of bricks were scattered by the explosions, but no one was hurt. The fire continued to burn throughout the morning. Many of those who came early stayed on, as more devastated members of the community came to see what was left of the building.

The older part of the high school had been built in 1896, with the newer section, where the fire began, added in 1910. This rare photograph shows not only the extent of the damage to the high school building but also the debris that was scattered by the explosions from the chemistry lab. (Courtesy Windham Historical Society.)

On the night of January 9, 1915, what was said to be "one of the most serious fires in a decade" occurred. The fire was discovered in the Natchaug Garage, directly in back of the Johnson House Hotel on Main Street. A fire alarm from Box 32 called out the three companies, and a general alarm was sounded immediately as soon as the firefighters saw the seriousness of the blaze.

The Natchaug Garage was destroyed in about 20 minutes. The east wall of the garage fell, allowing the fire to spread to the adjacent three-story Thread City garage, which was also destroyed along with several automobiles. After east wall of the Thread City garage fell, the intense heat threatened a nearby livery stable, 14 dwellings, and the Hooker House hotel.

On the south side of the garages, the fire spread to and gutted the Johnson House, a three-story wooden building on Main Street. Several other smaller buildings and sheds were destroyed as well. All 120 Willimantic firefighters were on the scene, and every hose line in the department was put to use. Hoses were also borrowed from the Holland Silk Company on Valley Street.

Through the night and into the next day, thousands of onlookers came from Willimantic and surrounding towns to assess the damage, which was estimated at $90,000, with another $150,000 worth of property threatened. Only the valiant efforts of the firefighters prevented several other buildings from catching.

Many people came to find out what had happened to their cars, as more than a dozen cars were burned. Among the cars lost were a Reo Touring car, an Oakland six-cylinder, and a five-passenger Cadillac. Here, one of the automobiles hangs from the second floor.

In 1887, Marshall Tilden bought and rebuilt a structure that was described as the most ornamental four-story block in the city. In May 1906, the Jordan Brothers purchased the Tilden Block for their growing hardware business. On the morning of November 23, 1916, the Tilden-Jordan Block was completely ruined by fire.

The Tilden-Jordan fire had begun in the adjacent Star Moving Picture Theatre. Fire chief Thomas P. Foley was awakened by the clapper in his room. When he got to the scene of the fire, he sent a firefighter to Bank Street to ring the alarm by hand.

All the fire companies responded to the alarm, but by then the fire had gained headway and had progressed into the Jordan Block. Throughout the early morning hours, firemen poured streams of water on the building and stayed on the scene until late in the evening.

At the time, the fire was the worst in the history of the city in terms of financial loss. The Jordans said their loss would be well over $150,000. Henry Fryer's tailoring establishment on the second floor was also wiped out. The Natchaug Lodge and the Thread City Cyclers also rented rooms in the building and suffered financial losses.

This photograph shows the Alert Hose Company hand-drawn wagon at the rear of the Jordan Block. Two days after the fire, the west wall collapsed at 11:00 a.m. A few minutes later, the east wall fell. Because of fears that the rear wall would collapse onto a passing train, dynamite was used to destroy it that day.

At 4:00 p.m. on November 25, 1916, the wall was dynamited. The explosion sent debris flying as far as the footbridge. Several people, including Mayor Daniel Dunn, were injured, and one person later died. This rare photograph shows the results of the dynamite explosion. The Turner Building on Main Street is in the distance.

On September 19, 1940, Bank Street headquarters received a phone call from a woman at 2:40 a.m., reporting that the whole Willimantic Lumber and Coal Company was on fire. When the firemen arrived on the scene, flames were shooting more than 100 feet in the air.

Stocks of paint and varnishes in the lumberyard drove the flames higher, constantly forcing the 125 firefighters back. The occupants of surrounding buildings started to remove valuables and all day, a crowd estimated to be in the thousands watched the fireman as they doused the flames.

The intense heat damaged several surrounding buildings and blistered structures on the opposite side of Church Street. Firemen constantly hosed the roofs of all surrounding structures, and saved a large number of buildings from greater damage. The sparks were a constant danger, and many were falling as far away as the Valley Street extension.

This photograph shows the extent of the destruction caused by the heat and flames spreading from the Lumber Company fire. The total damage done by the fire was estimated to be $125,000. It was the most disastrous fire in Willimantic since the Jordan Block fire in 1916.

Just before 4:00 a.m. on Sunday, August 29, 1943, nearby residents heard a "thunderous noise" from the vicinity of the State Normal School on Windham Street. Shortly thereafter, a telephone alarm, followed by a box alarm from Box 19, alerted firefighters of the fire, which ended up consuming the 48-year-old school in an inferno, with losses estimated at $200,000.

The first firefighters on the scene of the State Normal School fire encountered a mass of flames shooting as high as 50 feet in the air, making it impossible to save the furnishings or any of the 60,000 volumes in the library. Locomotive whistles from engines working at the railroad station attracted the attention of residents in the city and outlying towns, and soon hundreds of spectators were on hand.

Embers from the blaze were blown as far as five blocks away. Even though a recall was sounded about four hours after the fire began, firefighters were still pouring water on the ruins until late that afternoon. All that remained were the exterior walls.

Here, Willimantic Engine No. 1, a 1927 Mack AC Bulldog chain drive, operates at the Normal School fire as firefighters remain on the scene, pouring water on the smoldering remains of the building. It was common practice at the time to raise the hood in order to help cool the engine.

Late in the afternoon at the Normal School fire, Willimantic auxiliary firefighter Paul "Pop" Miller operates one of the V-8 pumps supplying water to the firefighters at the Normal School. The nearby Burr Hall Dormitory and several neighboring houses had to be protected from flames and heat after the residents were evacuated.

In December 1944, a fire gutted the Shea Block on the corner of Railroad and Main Streets. It was one of the oldest buildings on Main Street, built in 1862 and known for many years as the European House. The fire was called in by policeman Raymond Tatro, who pulled the box alarm from Lincoln Square—seen in the background with the lighted Christmas tree.

In October 1949, a fire ruined the third floor of the Sadd Block, caused water damage to second-floor apartments, and affected several businesses, including Sears-Roebuck, the Firestone Accessory Store, Phil Viens's barbershop, Dr. Hudson Barrows's optometric offices, and the offices of Dr. Thomas Keegan and attorney Alva P. Loiselle.

The two-alarm fire at the Sadd Block, which began around 8:00 p.m. and resulted in approximately $50,000 in damage, was brought under control in about an hour and a half. The Coventry, Eagleville, Mansfield, North Windham, and Windham Center fire departments were called in to assist and the state police assisted Willimantic police in handling the crowds.

On the morning of January 30, 1953, a resident of St. Mary's Court was awakened by a fire at St. Mary's School. At 3:58 a.m., the fire department was called. When they arrived at the school, fire chief Leo Rivard found most of the structure to be in flames and immediately put in a call for mutual aid from surrounding departments.

The fire burned out of control for almost five hours. The temperature was below freezing and a stiff wind carried smoke, sparks, and debris as far as Maple Avenue and Jackson Street, threatening both St. Joseph's School and St. Joseph's Convent. Willimantic's recently purchased aerial ladder was put to the test.

Fire officials said that the fire, which caused damage estimated at $300,000, originated in the school's boiler room. The original part of the St. Mary's School building dated back to the 1820s. The whole Willimantic community was shocked and responded to the need with a remarkable fundraising effort that led to the complete rebuilding of the school within two years.

On February 28, 1953, less than a month after the St. Mary's School fire, a fire ripped through Lindy's Restaurant and Milevitz's Clothing Store on Union Street, only a block away from St. Mary's. The fire started in the kitchen at Lindy's but spread quickly to the three second-floor apartments.

Responding to the box alarm around 8:00 a.m., firefighters found the building engulfed in flames. A strong wind fanned the flames, which gutted the top parts of the 2.5-story building. Residents lost most of their possessions. Fireman Francis O'Brien is at the top of the aerial ladder.

At the height of the blaze, firefighters rescued a 71-year-old man and carried him out of the second floor of the burning building. The damage was extensive in Milevitz's Clothing Store, although some of the stock was brought outside and covered with tarpaulins while firefighters battled the blaze.

In January 1954, a man on his way to church noticed a fire at Lounsbury's Garage at 1145 West Main Street. The man notified the fire department, which responded to the bell alarm at 6:00 a.m. The fire destroyed the garage, including the five trucks, two tractors, and $7,000 worth of tools inside. Here, Deputy chief Albert Martin oversees the firefighting.

The 40-foot-by-100-foot Lounsbury's Garage was engulfed in flames when firefighters arrived. Aided by firefighters from three surrounding towns, firefighters were able to save the nearby Leiss Velvet Company plant from damage.

Unfortunately, three firemen were hurt when a chimney fell during the fire, which caused $60,000 in damage. The most seriously hurt was firefighter Leo Theriault, who had to be extricated from the rubble and suffered a fractured spine and fractured ribs. His injuries were permanent. He had been appointed to the fire department after being awarded the Silver Star for gallantry in World War II.

One of the most memorable fires in the city's history was the Valentine's Day fire of 1968. The blaze started in the basement of the Sherwin Williams paint store and was fed by thousands of gallons of paint. The fire swept through and destroyed three buildings and damaged another. Here, firemen continue to spray streams of water onto the fire as dawn breaks.

Willimantic firefighters fight the Valentine's Day blaze from the rear of the involved buildings. In the subzero temperatures, water froze quickly and created treacherous conditions. The fire, which began about 1:40 a.m., was not declared under control until evening. Eventually, eight mutual aid fire companies were called in to help fight the blaze.

In 1969, after several years of preparation, the Willimantic Redevelopment Agency decided to go ahead with an $8-million program of redevelopment. One of the properties scheduled for demolition was the Central Building on Union Street. Two years later, the Central Building was still intact until the evening of Sunday, October 31, 1971, when a fire gutted the building and left 32 people homeless.

Fire chief Phil Valone, driving home on Main Street, observed heavy smoke from the area and radioed the fire department to ask if there had been any alarms. Just as he was told that no alarms had come in, a box alarm was rung. All personnel and equipment from Willimantic were summoned to the Central Building, as well as mutual aid from nine surrounding towns.

Chief Valone said the fire started in one of the second-floor apartments in the central part of the building, belonging to one of the six families occupying the two upper floors of the building. The blaze was brought under control in about two hours.

This photograph, looking east down Union Street, shows the extent of the firefighting operations on the street. The Central Building was a sprawling building with several additions added to it over the years on the corner of Union and Center Streets. Ladders and equipment were set up all along Center Street as well because the building was so large.

In the early morning hours of July 14, 1979, one of the approximately 20 persons in the Shell Chateau said he smelled smoke and the building was evacuated. Although the fire department were quick to respond, flames were already shooting through the roof and leaping into the air. Acting captain Joseph "Al" Beaulieu said the roof was "tinder dry" and "the fire was boiling under it."

The Shell Chateau was built in 1936 and named after a nearby gas station. Ironically, the "S" had dropped off the Shell Chateau sign here and, with the building engulfed in flames, it became exactly what the sign spelled out.

Acting captain Joseph "Al" Beaulieu, who was in charge of the firefighting effort, said the flames "had been going for quite some time in the loft," before it was discovered. The blaze was hard to contain because there were no firewalls. Firefighters had to cut holes in the roof in order to vent the flames, and the roof eventually caved in.

For a firefighter, nothing is worse than a fire causing a fatality. On February 21, 1987, five children under the age of two died as a fire gutted a West Avenue apartment. Firefighters tried valiantly to reach the children but were driven back by the intense heat. In this photograph, fire chief John Walsh talks with Willimantic police lieutenant Clifford Spinner. The faces of firefighters Jack Pickett (left) and Bert Koppisch show the emotional strain of the ordeal.

The firefighters were devastated by the tragedy. After spending time talking with his firefighters, Chief Walsh said, "No words can alleviate the feelings they have, it's the look on their faces." A fire chaplain and two other clergymen were at the scene to comfort family members, neighbors, and the distraught firefighters. "They tried their utmost," said Chief Walsh.

American Thread Company's Mill No. 4, when completed in the 1880s, was the largest mill in the world on one floor—840 feet long and 168 feet wide—and the first industrial building in the world to be lighted by electricity, some of which was designed by Thomas Edison himself. In July 1995, it was leveled by a massive arson fire that brought in departments from many locations and took over three days to finally extinguish.

Like many textile mills in New England, the American Thread Company was a major employer. It also helped give Willimantic the nickname Thread City. However, after the mills closed, they became targets for fires. Over the years, the floors had become soaked in oil and were disasters waiting to happen. Here, hose lines stretch across the bridge to the scene of the mill fire.

This aerial view of the American Thread mill fire shows the extent of the damage and the hose lines utilized to attack the fire.

Four
Service to the Community

The Willimantic firefighters do much more than fight fires and protect lives and property. The greatest percentage of calls received by the department are for medical emergencies, not just in Willimantic but throughout the town of Windham.

Throughout their history, they have also given of their time to the community in other ways, putting on dances and banquets and sponsoring fairs, parades, and sporting events. They have run up and down stairs for the Salvation Army, gotten dunked and collected "tolls" for the Muscular Dystrophy Association, and been covered with foam while supporting Fire Prevention Week.

The department has been the center for communications for surrounding towns. In 1952, the department installed a switchboard that coordinated the dispatching and firefighting efforts of 16 departments. On-duty firefighters manned the switchboard—Station WW—24 hours a day. It is thought to have been the first regional dispatch center in Connecticut.

Many firefighters have additional duties, acting as apparatus mechanics, alarm box technicians, and training instructors. The firefighters are members of the International Firefighter's Union Local 1033. Since 1949, the union has played an active role in numerous community functions, with firefighter members sponsoring youth baseball and football teams and supporting local charitable organizations. The firefighters have also published fire prevention material and informational material to acquaint people with the fire department and its role and history.

Mayor Florimond Bergeron (holding microphone) and fire chief Leo Rivard attend the July 1952 opening of the Mutual Aid Dispatch Center at the Bank Street headquarters. At its beginning, the new system linked 12 departments, allowing callers from all participating towns to call one telephone number to report emergencies.

The dispatch and switchboard center at the Bank Street headquarters, seen here in 1960, received calls and then notified the member town by activating its siren. If the town's resources were busy, other towns were notified as needed.

In cooperation with the fire department, local businesses distributed cards with the locations of all the department's Gamewell fire alarm boxes. This system was begun in 1877 at a cost of $400. Originally, it was connected to a bell at the Brainerd House hotel. The clerk there would then signal the mills to start their pumps and the firefighters to assemble.

BOX	LOCATION
12	West Main St. near residence of M. Rosen
121	Brown Ave.
13	West Main St. and Holbrook Avenue
14	Town Home, West Main St.
15	Main St., opp. Mansfield Avenue
152	Corner Birch and Valley Sts.
16	Vanderman's Foundry—Private
17	Corner Mansfield Ave. and Prospect St.
171	Community Hospital—Private
172	Quarry St., at Rosen St.
18	Mansfield Ave. and Summit St. exten.
21	Corner Bridge and Mountain Sts.
23	Corner Bridge and Pleasant Sts.
231	Corner Card and Pleasant Sts.
24	Corner Mountain and Pleasant Sts.
25	Corner Lebanon Ave. and Pleasant St.
27	Corner South and Pleasant Sts.
271	Corner John and So. Park Sts.
28	Corner South and Bain Sts.
31	Corner High and Main Sts.
32	Corner Walnut and Valley Sts.
33	Corner Windham and Valley Sts.
331	Model School
333	Teachers College Dormitory
34	Corner Main and Bank Sts.
35	Corner North and Valley Sts.
36	Connecticut Light and Power Co.—Private.
37	Lincoln's Sq.
371	Center St., opp. French Club
38	Corner Valley and Jackson Sts.

BOX	LOCATION
39	Main St., opp. Jackson St.
41	Corner Chestnut and Spring Sts.
42	Corner Church and Prospect Sts.
43	Corner Maple Ave. and Bellevue St.
44	High St., at Serwan Ave.
45	Corner High and Prospect Sts.
46	Corner Walnut and Summit Sts.
47	Corner Lewiston Ave. and North St.
48	Cor. Washburn and Walnut Sts.
51	Milk St., near Railroad Crossing
513	Roselin Mfg.—Private.
52	Corner Summit and Jackson Sts.
521	Oak and Prospect Sts.
53	Corner Carey and Jackson Sts.
531	Normandie Ave., opp. Terry Court
54	Corner Oak St. and Lewiston Ave.
55	Corner Ash and Jackson Sts.
56	Corner Ash and North Sts.
57	Friendship and Cross Sts.
61	Windham Road and Park St.
62	South Park St., opp. West Park St.
63	Windham Road, cor. Godfrey St.
64	Corner Fairview St. and Quercus Ave.
71	Junction Main and Union Sts., East
72	Chapman St., near Milk Depot
73	Main St., junction of Ash St.
74	Main St., opp. Beech St.
81	No. 1 Mill American Thread Co.—Private
82	No. 2 Mill American Thread Co.—Private
84	No. 4 Mill American Thread Co.—Private
85	No. 6 Mill American Thread Co.—Private

SIGNALS

1 One Stroke Calls Chief.
1-1 Two Strokes slowly; fire out or under control.
2-2 At 8:00 a. m., no school in the forenoon; same signal at 11:30 a. m., no school in the afternoon.
2-2 Off Platoon report to headquarters.
3-3 Call Engine Co. No. 1 and Truck No. 1 report at headquarters.
4-4 General Alarm.
10 Military Call; National Guard Co. report at the State Armory.

THE GERLACH-BARKLOW CO., JOLIET, ILL., U. S. A.

TELEPHONE CALLS

Chief, 1548. Engine Co. No. 1, 348.

INSTRUCTIONS

To send alarm, break glass, turn key to right and open door. Pull hook down as far as it will go ONCE and let go.

On the pull-down type of box, pull handle outward, then pull lever down ONCE and let go.

Remain at box until apparatus arrives to notify firemen of the location of the fire.

Signals will be given only by the Chief or Deputy-Chief.

AMOS E. BARBER, Chief.

In 1953, members of the fire department presented these gifts of a respirator and croupette to the Windham Community Memorial Hospital. The gifts were received by Charles W. Hill, hospital president, William B. Sweeney, administrator, and Dr. Sawyer E. Medbury. From left to right are (first row) William B. Sweeney, firefighter William Smith, Charles W. Hill, and Dr. Sawyer G. Medbury; (second row) firefighter George Taylor, Ambrose "Sam" Roy, Charles Kelley, George Thompson, deputy chief Albert Martin, Nelson Flagg, Chief Leo Rivard, and firefighter Francis O'Brien, president of the local firefighter's union.

Willimantic's first ambulance was a 1947 Ford donated by the Lion's Club. In the 1940s, after taking part in Red Cross training programs, the fire department began to respond to medical assistance calls, but they did not transport patients.

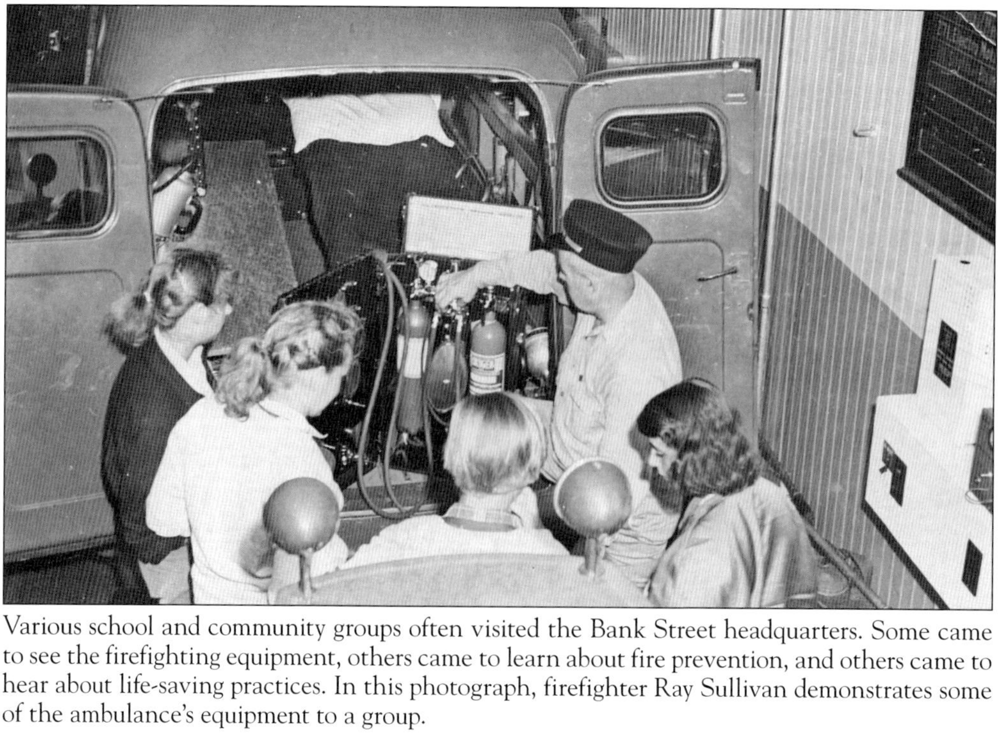

Various school and community groups often visited the Bank Street headquarters. Some came to see the firefighting equipment, others came to learn about fire prevention, and others came to hear about life-saving practices. In this photograph, firefighter Ray Sullivan demonstrates some of the ambulance's equipment to a group.

This ambulance was originally donated to Windham Hospital by the Lion's Club. After the hospital stopped providing ambulance service, the fire department took over the service. By 1956, the ambulance was also used for mutual aid calls. The very night that the mutual aid plan was agreed upon, ambulances from the fire department, the hospital, and Lebanon were called to a serious accident.

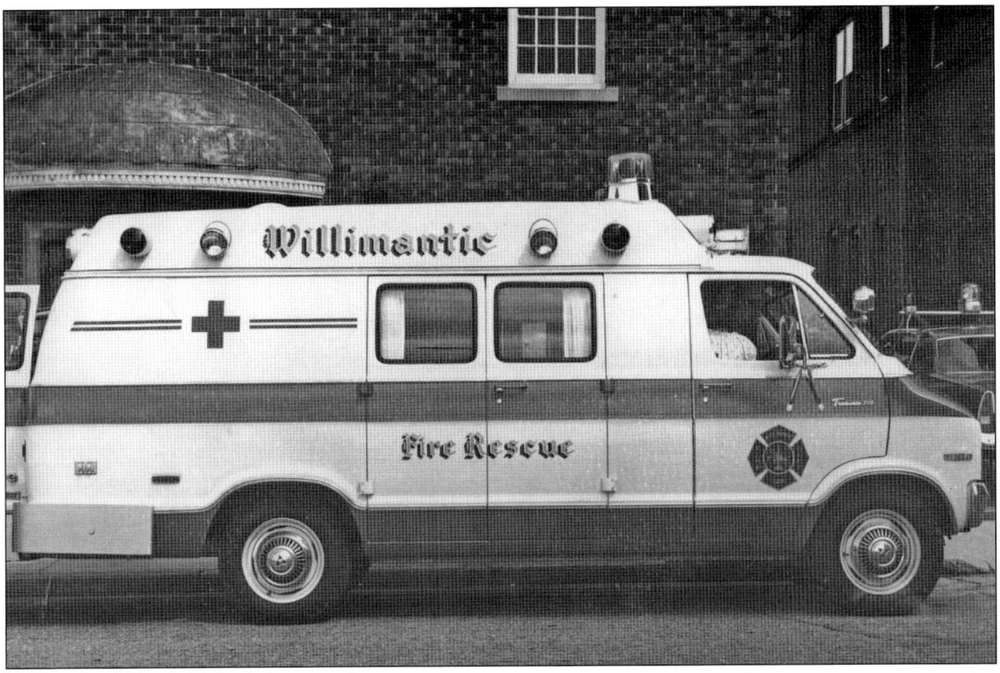

Prior to this new, van-style vehicle, the Willimantic Fire Department, like many others, used a low-profile Cadillac ambulances. These vehicles had no headroom and no working area for the attendants. With the introduction of these van-style ambulances, firefighters and emergency medical technicians could care for patients better.

Fire department members and city leaders gather to take delivery of their new van-style ambulance. They are, from left to right, city councilman Richard Nassiff, Robert Gorgone, Joe DeMarchi, Capt. George Taylor, Anthony Santa Lucia, and Mayor David Calchera.

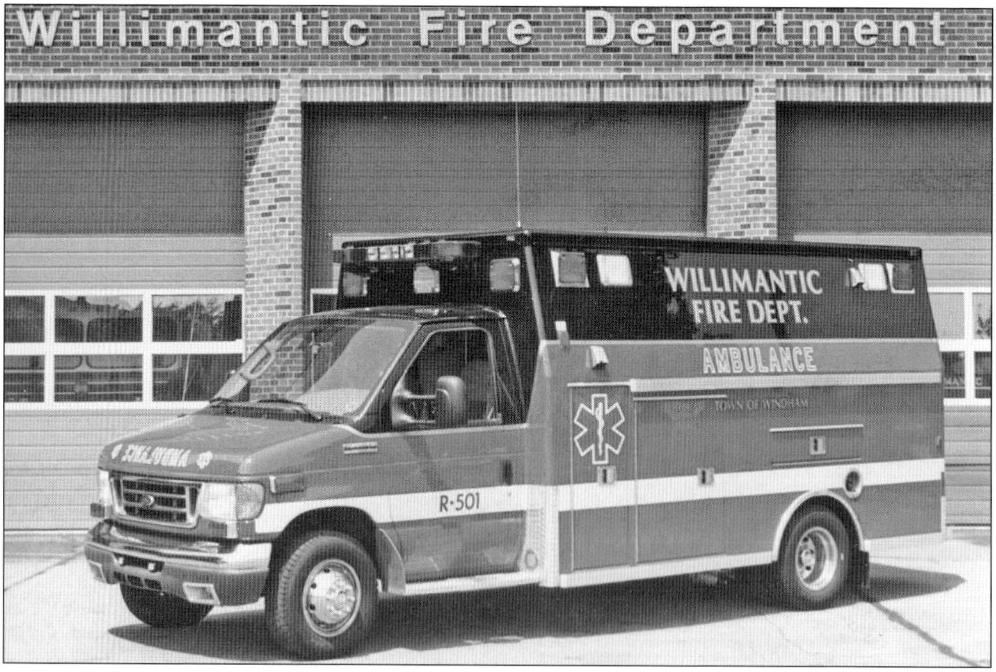

Rescue 501, a 2007 ambulance, shows the progression from the 1947 rescue truck to the 1967 low-profile Cadillac, to the van-style ambulance for improved patient care, and on to the new large, box-sized ambulances with the most advanced emergency care equipment. In Willimantic, between 75 and 80 percent of the department calls are for medical assistance.

In the early 1960s, the Firefighters Local 1033 assisted the Salvation Army's coffee fund by donating a coffee machine and several cans of coffee. The funds for the donation came from the first-annual Firemen's Ball. Pictured from left to right are firefighters Ambrose Roy, William Smith, Phil Valone, Paul "Pop" Miller, and Capt. John E. Trask from the Salvation Army.

In the late 1970s, the Community Development Agency passed out free smoke detectors to low-income residents. The detectors were then installed by Willimantic firefighters. Many of the units were installed in city housing developments. Here, firefighter Joseph Marsalisi (on ladder) and two unidentified firefighters install one of the detectors.

In this fire-prevention photograph from the early 1970s, firefighter Robert Gorgone is covered with what is called Hi-Expansion foam by firefighter Ray Crosthwaite, using a special foam nozzle. The foam gives the impression of someone being covered by an out-of-control bubble bath, and the children from Natchaug School are justifiably impressed.

In this late 1970s photograph, everybody's favorite firefighting bear, Smokey—in this case, firefighter Joseph "Al" Beaulieu—and Susie the fire dog sit atop the aerial ladder as they prepare to participate in the annual Fire Prevention Parade. Like departments all over the country, Willimantic firefighters increase their fire prevention efforts during the weeks of October set aside for it by the National Fire Prevention Association.

Fire chief Albert Martin (left) and deputy chief Ambrose "Sam" Roy are with schoolchildren during Fire Prevention Week. The department would hold an open house for the week and invite children to visit to learn safety tips, see demonstrations and receive plastic firefighter helmets.

Firefighter Jim Jensen speaks about fire safety with a group of kindergarten children in the 1990s. During Fire Prevention Weeks, it was not unusual for hundreds of students to be brought to the firehouse by their teachers.

Here again, more fire prevention efforts are offered by firemen. Deputy chief and fire marshal Richard Miller awards prizes to some lucky schoolchildren for their participation in the department's fire prevention poster contest. The grand prize was a bicycle, and the other prizes were smoke detectors for the home.

During Fire Prevention Weeks, Willimantic firefighters travel to many schools to speak about fire safety. Many other groups and classes come to the firehouse. In the upstairs rooms of the firehouse, there are countless photographs of firefighters with classes they hosted and notes of thanks from happy children.

Fire-prevention awareness is demonstrated here by firefighter Nick Lucas, who is showing young children how a smoke detector works and why it is important for families to have them in their homes. Along with the lecture, important information was also given to the youngsters to be brought home to their parents.

For many years, the fire department has participated in fundraising events to support the Muscular Dystrophy Association. In this photograph, fire chief Charles Monzillo gets dunked as part of a fundraising activity. In the background is firefighter Roy Dingler. Everyone got into the act during these annual fundraising efforts.

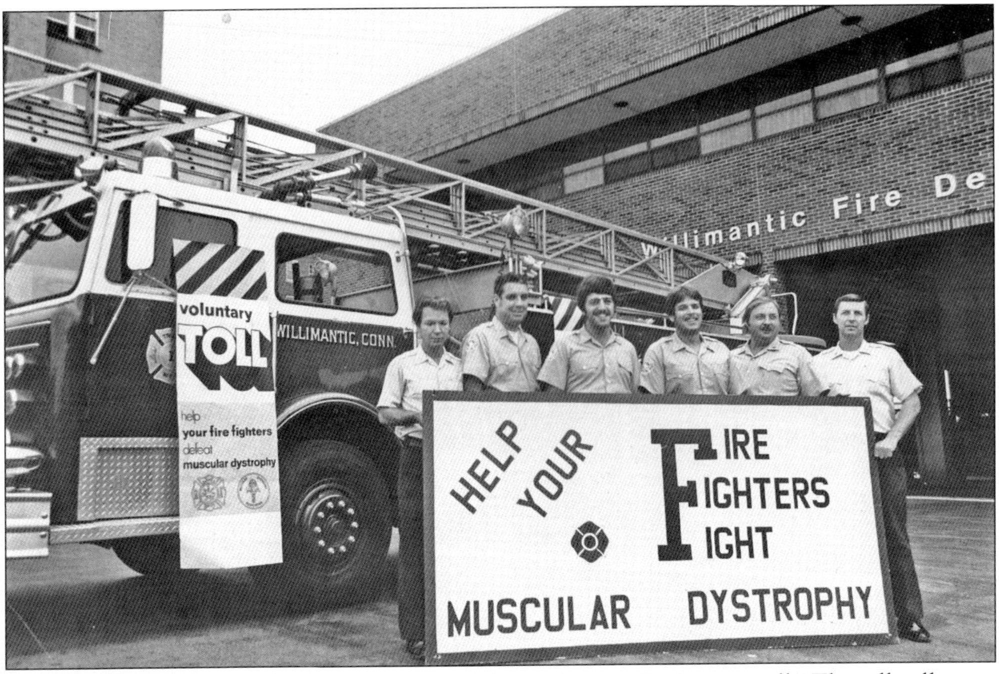

In the 1980s, Willimantic firefighters stationed themselves at a "voluntary toll." The toll collectors shown here are Capt. Burt Koppisch and firefighters Jack Pickett, Jim Jensen, Roy Dingler, Joseph "Al" Beaulieu, and Capt. Milton Shippee.

In 1994, Capt. Joe DeMarchi carried the oldest of three children to safety through deep snow after water pipes froze in the house and the family's apartment was flooded.

Sled 1 (above) was originally fitted out for use in snow-covered areas that would be difficult for ambulances to reach. The sled and snowmobile above were housed at the Bank Street headquarters but were available for all area departments. During the blizzard of 1978, it was used to rescue a man suffering a heart attack, saving his life.

The Salvation Army has been there for the fire department, especially at fire scenes, where they have supplied hot drinks and snacks. In turn, the fire department has been there for the Salvation Army, helping with the Kettle Drive and doing the Staircase Climb, which firefighters Mike Bergeron (left) and Nick Lucas are doing here in the 1980s at Eastern Connecticut State University.

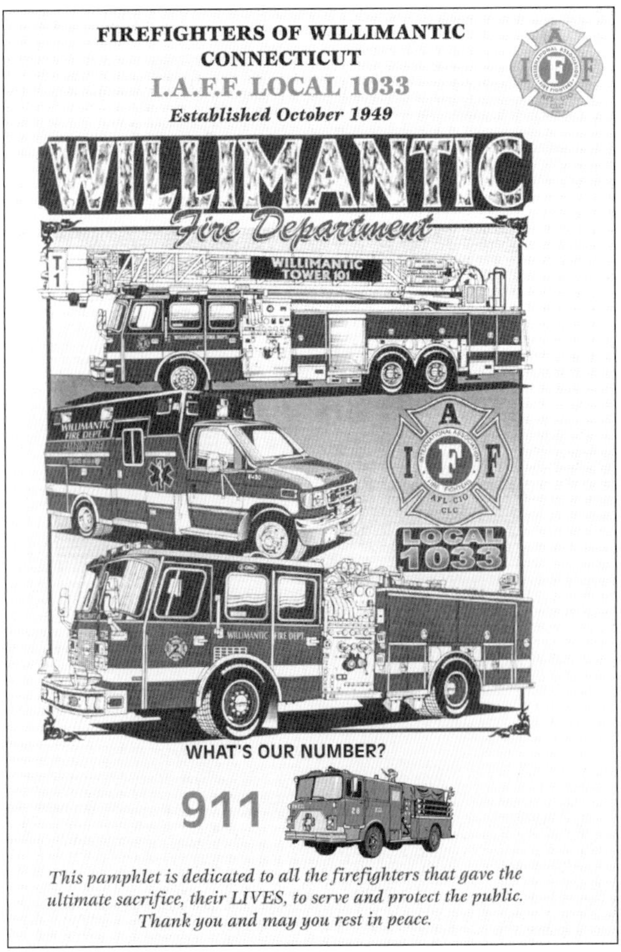

Above, Willimantic firefighters respond to a car-versus-tree accident on Bricktop Road in September 1995. The accident was considered to be weather-related and the injuries were minor. The fire department provides fire-based ambulance service to the approximately 17,000 residents in the entire town of Windham with only two ambulances.

The Willimantic Firefighters Union published this informational booklet about the fire department. It provided a short history of the fire department, facts about the present-day department, and a chart detailing the responses it made. It also contained safety rules and a question-and-answer section that explained fire equipment, what firefighters do when not responding to emergencies, and what personnel do at a fire scene.

Five

Between the Alarms

For many, the life of a firefighter can be 90 percent boredom, followed by 10 percent excitement. However, that time "between the alarms" takes on a life of its own. The Willimantic firefighters have shown that there is a lot more to their job than fighting fires and responding to medical emergencies. The get-togethers, firefighters' memorial celebrations, balls, and sporting events, and the camaraderie and antics of the clowns show that there was, is, and always will be a lot going on between the alarms.

Like many fire departments across America, the dog, particularly the dalmatian, was an integral part of the fabric of firefighting life. In the early, horse-drawn days, these dogs would run ahead of the engines, warning the public. As fire engines became motorized, the dogs took their place riding on the rigs. The Willimantic Fire Department has had several mascots, from the mascots of the Hilltop and Alert Hose companies to Duke, Susie, and Lucky from the 1950s to the 1990s.

Lucky was found by a canine control officer in another town. No one claimed the dog, and he was going to be put down. The canine officer, a volunteer firefighter, could not let this happen, so he brought the dog to Willimantic, and the rest, as they say, is history. Retired chief John Walsh remembers Lucky's ability to escape the firehouse, walk several blocks to the local grocery store, wait for someone to activate the automatic door, walk in to the store, and abscond with a package of steak from the meat counter.

Firefighters get together for a dinner at the Bank Street headquarters in the 1940s. The only identifiable members are Steve Sabo (left side of table, third down), Mayor Florimond Bergeron (upper left corner), fire chief Leo Rivard (right side of table, second from the end), Lieutenant Sullivan (all the way down in front), and deputy chief Albert Martin (standing against the pole).

Firefighters have dinner together in the 1950s. From the front left side of the table clockwise are George Farley, Al Martin, two unidentified men, fire chief Leo Rivard, Lieutenant Sullivan, William Smith, unidentified, Paul "Pop" Miller, George Menditto, and Francis O'Brien.

In this late 1940s photograph, a group of firefighters, auxiliary members, and a call man or two play cards during downtime at the Bank Street headquarters. Lieutenant Sullivan is in the light-colored uniform. William Smith is standing by, observing, and maybe kibitzing a little.

The salute ceremony concludes the grand march at the beginning of this 1950s Firemen's Ball. Pictured are Russell Taylor, Helen Valone, Phillip Valone, unidentified MC, Paul "Pop" Miller, Josephine Martin, deputy chief Albert Martin, Barbara Roy, Ambrose "Sam" Roy, Florina Bergeron, Florimond Bergeron, guest of Chief Rivard, Chief Leo Rivard, Bernice O'Brien (partially hidden), and Francis O'Brien.

Firefighters read the Fireman's Prayer at a memorial Sunday service in the 1970s. From left to right are Joseph "Al" Beaulieu, Jack Pickett, Chris Beaulieu (the son of Joseph "Al" Beaulieu), Ron Palmer Jr., Ron Palmer Sr., Anthony Santa Lucia, Rick Nadeau, Dave Maynard, retired chief Albert Martin, Capt. Milt Shippee. Behind Captain Shippee is Capt. James Connell, and in the background are firefighters John Griffin and Joseph Marsalisi.

Seen at a Sunday memorial service in the 1980s are, from left to right, fire chief John Walsh, Capt. James Connell, Dave Maynard, Gary Gorgone, Rick Nadeau, Joseph "Al" Beaulieu, and Capt. Milt Shippee. Widows of former firefighters place flowered wreaths on the memorial.

Willimantic firefighters dressed as clowns prepare to participate in a parade in Lebanon. From left to right are Joseph "Al" Beaulieu, Ed Lussier, Bobby Theriault, Anthony Santa Lucia, and Jimmy Connell (sitting on the running board)

Willimantic firefighters participate in a Lebanon parade. From left to right are Robert Theriault, Larry Lemire, Congressman Robert Steele, Paul Bachand, Anthony Santa Lucia, Robert Pisicitello (kneeling), and Joseph "Al" Beaulieu. The firefighters/clowns participated in numerous parades and events to raise funds for the Muscular Dystrophy Association.

In this 1967 photograph, members of the Willimantic Fire Department, masquerading as clowns, prepare for a parade in Lebanon. From left to right are Joseph "Al" Beaulieu, Ed Lussier, Bob Theriault, Tony Santa Lucia, and Jim Connell. Several other members of the department were part of this clown contingent on other occasions and events, such as on Fire Prevention Weeks and especially during fundraisers for the Muscular Dystrophy Association.

Here, Willimantic firefighters participate in Plainfield's annual Victory over Japan Day Parade. From left to right are Chief Monzillo, Nick Lucas (pushing the "fire truck"), Rick Nadeau (with cigar), and Joseph "Al" Beaulieu (with umbrella). The youngster in the driver's seat is Nick Lucas's son Jon.

Proud firefighters John Beck and Nick Lucas stand by one of the original hose wagons, which they restored. It had been in the basement of the old Bank Street firehouse, and Lucas decided to restore it for the Windham Tercentenary. He did the rest of the metal repair, fabrication, lettering, and added the gold leaf. Beck also helped with painting and they pulled it in the Tercentenary Parade.

Firefighter John Griffin, with the mascot, Lucky, hands out some reading material during Fire Prevention Week. It was a common practice for firefighters—often accompanied by their mascot—to take one of their pieces of equipment to various locations in Willimantic. Hundreds of people would stop by to ask questions, sit in the driver's seat, and ring the bell as a firefighter passed out literature.

Willimantic firefighters encourage citizens to visit the firehouse to see the equipment and meet their firefighters. Even between the alarms, firefighters busy themselves with a multitude of duties. However, they are never too busy to spend time with visitors. Here, an obviously happy group of schoolchildren poses with Willimantic firefighters, from left to right, Jim Phillips, Evan Degatino, and Ron Miles Sr.

Members of the Hill Top Hose Company No. 3 gather in 1908 for a formal photograph. In front is the company mascot.

Susie, the fire department mascot, sits at the radio console in the Bank Street headquarters, and looks ready to give out a radio message for all to hear. Firefighters laughingly said that Susie manned the switchboard when they were away. Susie was four years old when this photograph was taken.

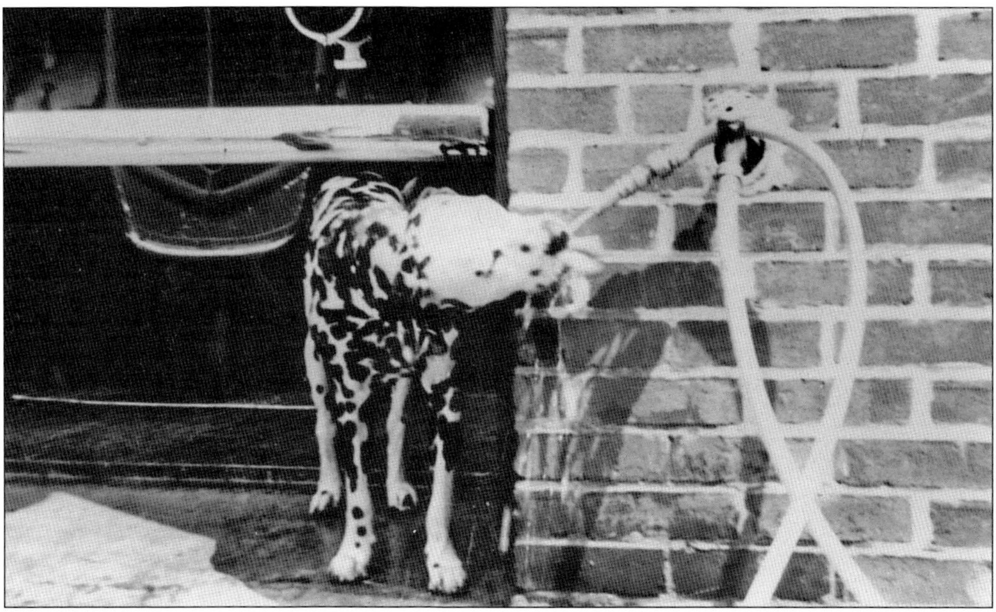

Duke became the fire department mascot in 1948. He rode to every alarm and was a beloved companion to the firefighters in their off-duty hours. He was also a mascot to their softball team and went to every game, home and away. In this 1950s photograph, Duke takes a well-deserved drink from the outside garden hose that someone must have left on for him.

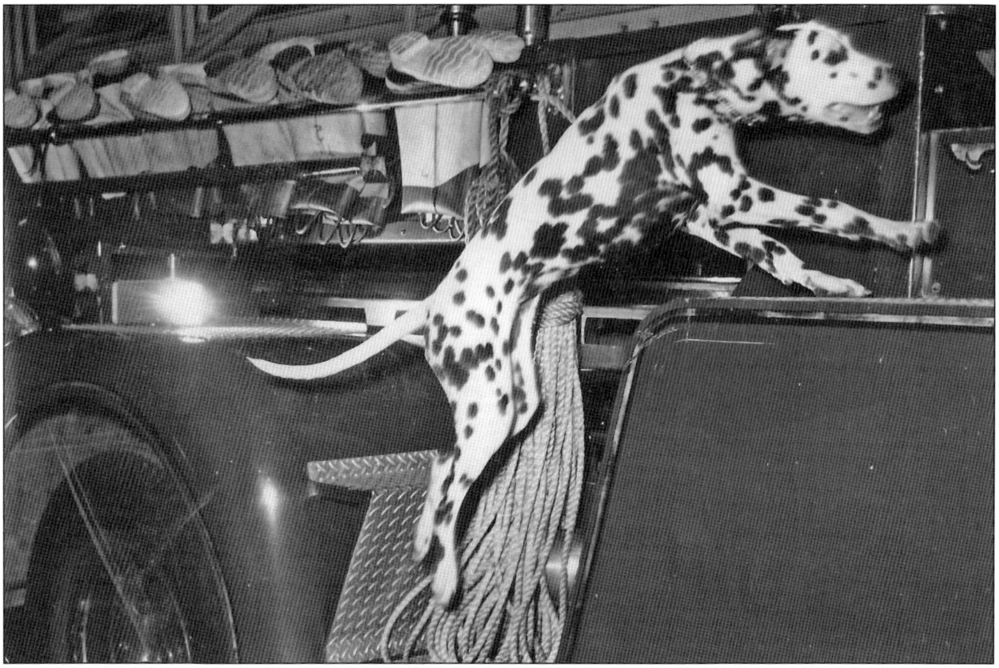

Firefighters reminiscing about Susie recalled that when she first came to the firehouse, she did not like the noise of the sirens from the fire apparatus, so would hide when the alarm went off. However, she loved the fire apparatus. Here, a nimble Susie jumps on to Aerial 1. There is an advantage to having an open cab fire truck, at least for Susie.

Susie the fire dog shows off her climbing abilities. Retired captain Ed Lussier remembers one time when he was hanging Christmas decorations on the old firehouse, he turned around to see Susie behind him watching. The only problem was that Susie could not climb down the aerial and needed his help.

Susie the dog happily lounges on the turntable of Willimantic Truck 101 in front of the Amercian Thread mill, surveying the crowd and waiting for a parade to start in the late 1960s. With Susie are Eddie Lussier (in the passenger seat) and fire chief Ambrose "Sam" Roy.

In this 1960s photograph, firefighter Francis Shea and Susie appear to be enjoying some time together sitting at the department's card table. (Photograph courtesy of Francis Shea.)

Firefighters said Susie could ruin a group tour because kids would stop following the tour so they could pet her. Here, Susie sits on her favorite chair on Halloween night and greets trick-or-treaters at the firehouse.

This is an iconic image of Susie sitting in front of Aerial 1 at fire headquarters. Susie was not only a mascot; she was a watchdog who guarded the firehouse while the firefighters slept. Susie died after 11 years of service and firefighters will always remember "the wonderful years of friendship" she gave to the department members.

Six

The Men and Women of the Department

Until recently, Willimantic, like many fire departments, was a man's bastion. For these men, this was their second home. They ate, worked, and slept in the same building, sometimes for days at a time. Many of these men had even spent time in the war together. They formed a bond that lasted for the rest of their lives.

Later, with the introduction of women into the fire service, they too worked, laughed, and lived within this group, adding their own spice to the mix. When looking at these photographs, old and new, there is an expression on all of their faces, an expression of satisfaction, determination, humor, and pride. Any firefighter looking at these images will recognize that look. The children and significant others of firemen know that look too. For those of you who have never seen that look, this chapter is for you.

A group of Willimantic firefighters stand in front of the 1940s-era Maxim fire engine and the auxiliary vehicle. Two of these firefighters eventually rose to the rank of fire chief. From left to right are Lt. Leo Rivard, who became chief in the late 1950s, unidentified, Paul "Pop" Miller, fire chief Amos Barber, Nelson Flagg, and Phil Valone, who became chief in the 1970s.

Another group of firefighters poses outside the Bank Street headquarters in the 1940s. From left to right are (kneeling) Lt. Ambrose Roy, Francis O'Brien, Paul Miller, and Duke the fire dog; (standing) deputy chief Albert Martin, fire chief Leo Rivard, Nelson Flagg, Charles Kelley, William Smith, and Phil Valone.

In the 1950s, the Willimantic firefighters ballclub (above) included, from left to right, (first row) Francis O'Brien, Pat Cormier, Duke the fire dog, Walter Safin, and Charles Sanborn; (second row) Paul Miller, W. Theriault, J. Commerford, and Phil Valone; (third row) four unidentified men and Steve Sabo (far right).

This candid image shows two Willimantic firefighters enjoying a joke or two. Both of these men would later become fire chief. Ambrose "Sam" Roy (left) was fire chief from 1969 to 1970, and Al Martin was chief from the early 1960s until 1969. In 1968, Chief Martin and then-deputy chief Roy oversaw what was reported to be the largest fire in memory, which struck downtown Willimantic on Valentine's Day.

This is a stylized composite of the Engine No. 2 crew. Like the other engine company crews or platoons, this group of men were a family unto themselves, which was a desirable situation for working together and imperative during fires and other emergencies. These men needed to depend on each other. Clockwise from bottom left are Francis O'Brien, Paul "Pop" Miller, Lt. Raymond Sullivan, William Smith, and George Menditto.

This 1950s photograph shows, from left to right, Bill Nichols, Lt. Raymond Sullivan, George Thompson, Pat Cormier, and Russell Taylor in front of fire headquarters on Bank Street, between Engine No. 3, and the auxiliary vehicle. This group includes two future chiefs and two captains. George Thompson and Lieutenant Sullivan became captains, and Bill Nichols and Patrick Cormier became chiefs.

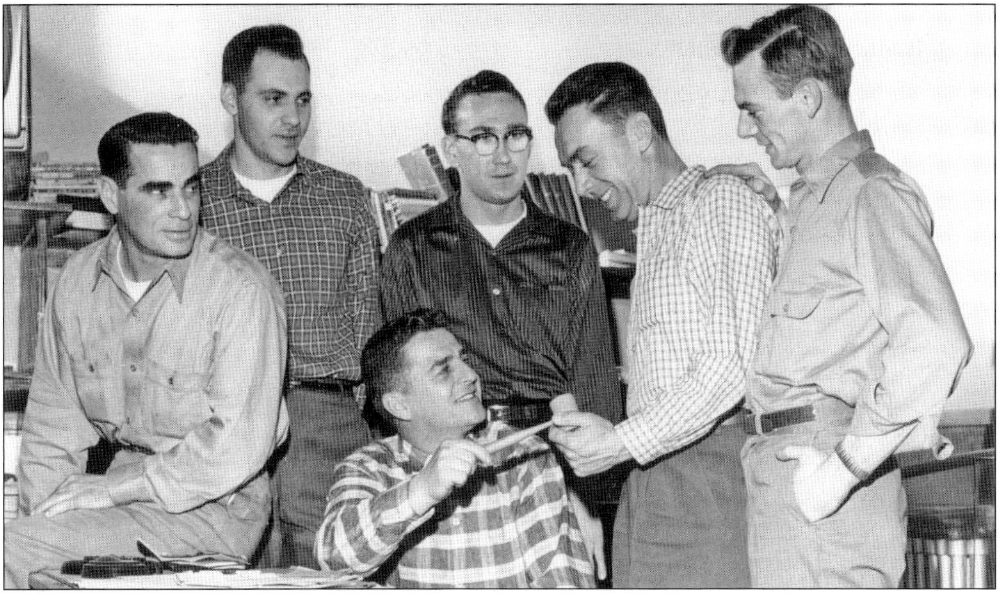

In January 1959, fire department members installed new officers for the Firefighters Union Local 1033. From left to right are George Menditto, treasurer Joseph Marsalisi, vice president Richard Miller, president Pat Cormier, and secretary George Taylor. Sitting is Walter Safin. For many years, the union held an annual banquet at fire headquarters in January, when officers were elected and installed.

In this 1973 photograph, members of Platoon 4 pose in their dress uniforms in front of the 1970 Maxim Engine. From left to right are Anthony Santa Lucia, Paul Bachand, Robert Theriault, Capt. Patrick Cormier, Joseph "Al" Beaulieu, Joseph DeMarchi, and Eddie Lussier. Not long after this, Captain Cormier became deputy chief, and later chief. Firefighters Beaulieu, DeMarchi, and Lussier also later became captains.

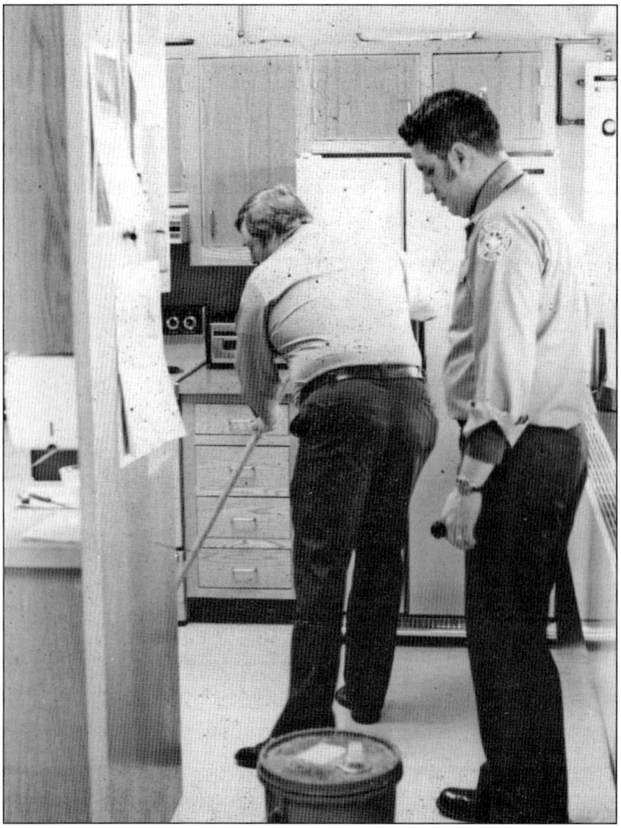

At the new fire station in the late 1970s are, from left to right, Robert Theriault, John Griffin, and Anthony Santa Lucia. It is unusual to see Tony Santa Lucia without his trademark cigar. Theriault is a second-generation Willimantic firefighter whose father was injured in a fire in the 1950s. Robert's son Kevin is now a captain in the department.

At left, Joseph "Al" Beaulieu and Jack Pickett wax the kitchen floor in the new fire headquarters in the 1980s. Unlike schools and stores, which hire janitors that do the light maintenance and housekeeping, firefighters are expected to keep up the appearances of their home away from home. Eventually, Beaulieu moved up the line and became a captain, leaving his waxing days behind him.

A group of Willimantic firefighters takes a break from their efforts to contain a massive fire at American Thread Company's Mill No. 4 in 1996. This mill fire took the resources of all of the Willimantic Fire Department and countless other town fire companies. Seen here from left to right are Alberto Torres, Scott Ellis, Capt. Nick Lucas, and Andrea Gamache.

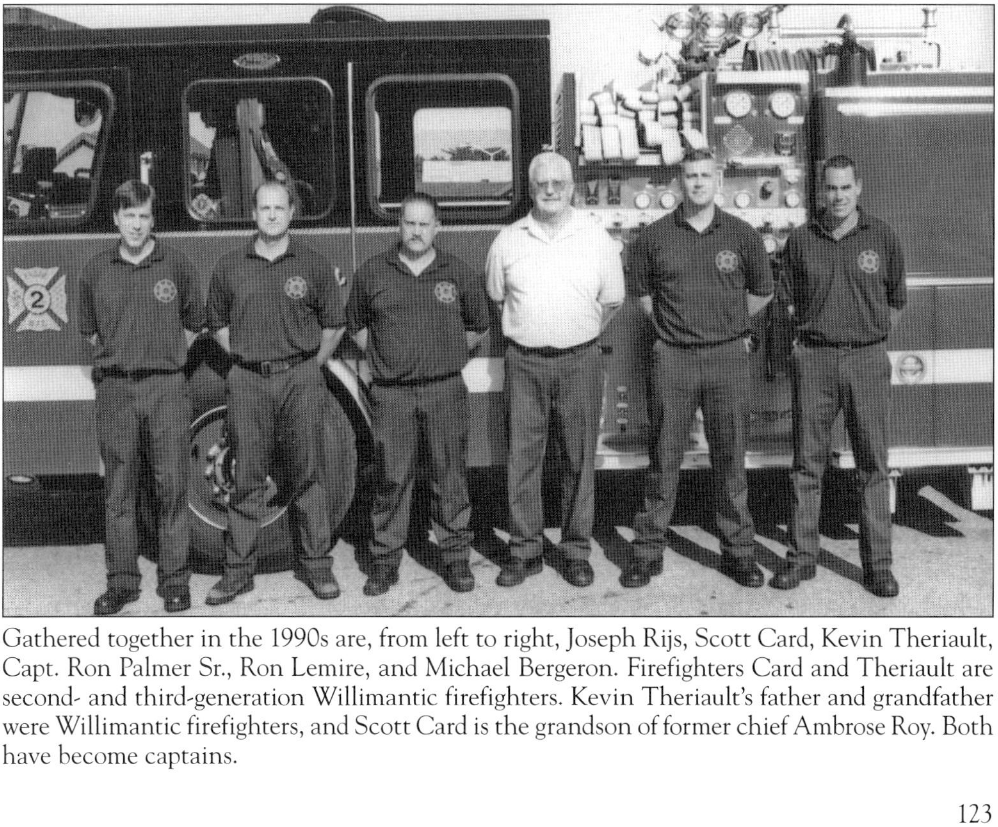

Gathered together in the 1990s are, from left to right, Joseph Rijs, Scott Card, Kevin Theriault, Capt. Ron Palmer Sr., Ron Lemire, and Michael Bergeron. Firefighters Card and Theriault are second- and third-generation Willimantic firefighters. Kevin Theriault's father and grandfather were Willimantic firefighters, and Scott Card is the grandson of former chief Ambrose Roy. Both have become captains.

In 1990, Platoon 2 posed for this photograph. They are, from left to right, Joseph DeMarchi, Robert Gorgone, Capt. Bert Koppisch, John Griffin, David Maynard, and James Jensen. For many years, Willimantic was a three-shift department, with each shift working eight hours. Later, the department went to a four-platoon system, with each platoon doing 10-hour day shifts and 14-hour night shifts.

After a 1992 fire at Young's Package Store when they had to deal with bitterly cold temperatures and icy conditions, (from right to left) Capt. Ron Palmer Sr., Mike Bergeron, and Nick Lucas posed for this photograph. The expression of satisfaction on the faces of the three tells it all. Although tired, wet, and dirty, the three men are proud of the job they have done.

Above, firefighter Alberto Torres, Capt. Joseph "Al" Beaulieu, and firefighter Holly Swiney are seen here at a minor fire started by a gas grill at a house on lower Main Street in 1998. Torres made department history in 1993 by becoming Willimantic's first Latino firefighter. In his first act as a firefighter, he extinguished a small blaze at a Jackson Street residence started by, of all things, a faulty smoke detector.

Firefighter Holly Swiney and a young student do a little fire hose training during the annual fire prevention demonstration at the fire headquarters. Holly Swiney demonstrates to this youngster how it feels to hold a charged hose line—albeit, not at full pressure and without flames raging. Willimantic holds these annual demonstrations to illustrate the work firefighters do.

As in many other jobs, there are maintenance chores to be done, and spring cleaning at the Willimantic firehouse is no different than in any other place, although the methods might be a little different. Here, firefighters Peter Bruscato (left) and Jim Soler utilize one of the fire department's pieces of apparatus to do a good job washing the outside windows of the fire headquarters.

Three Willimantic firefighters participate in training at the Eastern Connecticut Firemen's Training School in Willimantic. The school has educated hundreds of Eastern Connecticut firefighters in various methods of fire suppression, fire investigation, and hazardous material training. Many Willimantic firefighters have trained at this location. Seen here from left to right are Ron Lemire, Ron Palmer Jr., and Jim Soler.

Firefighters Ron Lemire and Scott Card undergo firefighter training at the Eastern Connecticut Firemen's Training School. In 1954, the Windham and Tolland County Firemen's Association endorsed the idea for the school and it opened that June with a parade of fire apparatuses going from Memorial Park to the site of the school. Deputy chief Albert Martin was the first instructor.

Celebrating at this preretirement dinner for firefighter Robert Gorgone are, from left to right, (sitting) Dave Maynard, Aron Buch, Robert Gorgone, and Ron Palmer Jr.; (standing) Chris Withington, Andrea McDevitt, and Capt. Nick Lucas.

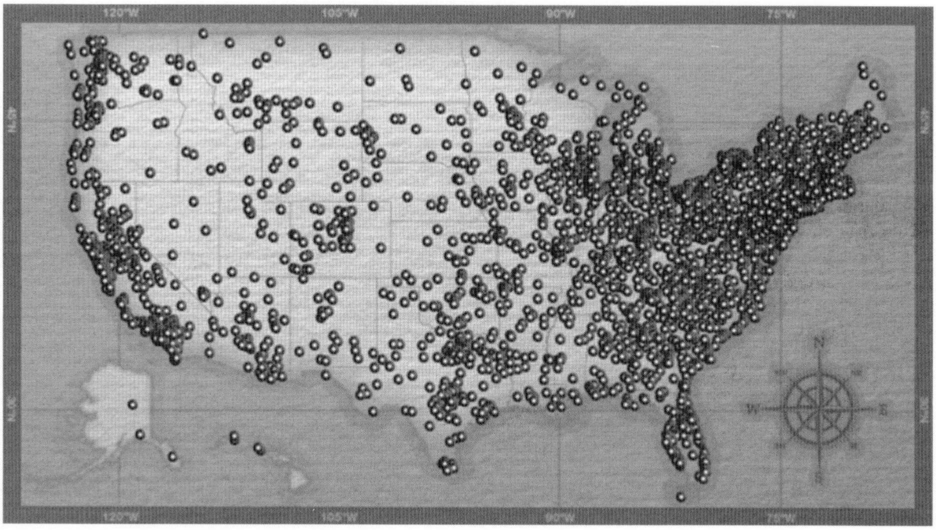